VIETNAM
Why We Fought

VIETNAM
Why We Fought

AN ILLUSTRATED HISTORY

DOROTHY and THOMAS HOOBLER

ALFRED A. KNOPF 🐎 NEW YORK

Grateful acknowledgment is made to the following for permission
to reprint previously published material:

Associated Press Newsfeatures: Excerpt from a letter by Robert Feltzer from an Associated Press article.
Reprinted by permission of the Associated Press. Fall River Music, Inc.: Excerpt from the lyrics to
"Where Have All the Flowers Gone?" by Pete Seeger. Copyright © 1961 by Fall River Music, Inc. All
rights reserved. Used by permission. Harcourt Brace Jovanovich, Inc., and Jonathan Cape Ltd.: Excerpts from *A Vietcong Memoir* by Truong Nhu Tang, David Chanoff, and Doan Van Toai. Copyright ©
1985 by Truong Nhu Tang, David Chanoff, and Doan Van Toai. Reprinted by permission of Harcourt
Brace Jovanovich, Inc., and Jonathan Cape Ltd. The New York Vietnam Veterans' Memorial Com-
mission: Excerpts from two letters from *Dear America: Letters Home from Vietnam,* edited by Bernard
Edelman (W. W. Norton, 1985; Pocket Books, 1986). Copyright © by The New York Vietnam Veter-
ans' Memorial Commission. Newsweek, Inc.: Excerpt from a *Newsweek* article of November 22, 1982.
Copyright © 1982 by Newsweek, Inc. All rights reserved. Reprinted by permission. Random House,
Inc., and Georges Borchardt, Inc.: Excerpts from *Portrait of the Enemy* by David Chanoff and Doan Van
Toai. Copyright © 1986 by David Chanoff and Doan Van Toai. Reprinted by permission of Random
House, Inc., Georges Borchardt, Inc., and the authors. Warner/Chappell Music, Inc.: Excerpt from the
lyrics to "Ballad of a Thin Man" by Bob Dylan. Copyright © 1965 by Warner Bros., Inc. All rights
reserved. Used by permission.

Photo research by the authors.

Cover photo credits: Front (clockwise from top): U.S. Air Force; U.S. Marine Corps; U.S. Army; U.S.
Navy; The Bettmann Archive. Back (clockwise from top): U.S. Marine Corps; The Bettmann Archive;
Army News Features; U.S. Army; U.S. Navy; Novosti from Sovfoto; The Bettmann Archive.
Text photo credits: 1, Werner Bischof/Magnum; 47, The Bettmann Archive; 165, Nick Sebastian/Black
Star; 189, AP/Wide World. All other credits appear in captions throughout.

THIS IS A BORZOI BOOK PUBLISHED BY ALFRED A. KNOPF, INC.

Copyright © 1990 by Dorothy and Thomas Hoobler. Maps copyright ©
1990 by Jim Kemp and Anita Karl. All rights reserved under International and Pan-American Copyright Conventions. Published in the United
States by Alfred A. Knopf, Inc., New York, and simultaneously in Canada
by Random House of Canada Limited, Toronto. Distributed by Random
House, Inc., New York. Manufactured in the United States of America.
Book design by Mina Greenstein.
10 9 8 7 6 5 4 3 2 1

Library of Congress Cataloging in Publication Data
Hoobler, Dorothy. Vietnam, why we fought / by Dorothy and Thomas
Hoobler. p. cm. Includes bibliographical references. Summary: Exam-
ines the history of Vietnam's relations with other nations, the involvement of the United States in the conflict, and the effects of the war.
1. Vietnamese Conflict, 1961–1975—United States—Juvenile literature.
2. Vietnam—History—Juvenile literature. [1. Vietnamese Conflict,
1961–1975. 2. Vietnam—History.] I. Hoobler, Thomas. II. Title.
DS558.H65 1990 959.704'3373—dc20 89-71645
ISBN 0-394-81943-8 (trade) ISBN 0-394-91943-2 (lib. bdg.)

Contents

Acknowledgments

The authors would like to thank everyone who helped us in collecting photographs for this book. Special thanks are due to Elvis Brathwaite of Wide World Photos, Dorothy McConchie at the Defense Department, Ronald W. Brenne of the United Press International Photo Library, Ann Stewart of Black Star, Annelise Hollman and Katherine Papparizos of the Public Information Service of the United Nations High Commission for Refugees, Rainaldo Reyes at the United Nations, Lynn Bowy of Magnum Photos, Catherine Cheval of Roger-Viollet, and Ha Huy Thong at the Vietnam Mission to the United Nations. Thanks also to J. Tuyet Nguyen for helping with the pronunciation of foreign names.

To our editor, Reg Kahney, we owe more than we can fully express. Her enthusiasm, encouragement, and energy carried the book—and its authors—through the completion of the writing. Her queries, suggestions, and ideas helped us to clarify the story of the Vietnam War. If the book succeeds in that aim, a large share of the credit should go to Reg and to Knopf's devotion to excellence. Of course, any errors in the book are our own.

The War at a Glance

111 B.C.	Vietnam becomes part of Chinese Empire.
A.D. 938	Battle of Bach Dang River—Vietnamese defeat Chinese fleet and win independence.
1863	France takes area around Saigon as a colony.
1884	All of Vietnam becomes a colony of France.
1890	Ho Chi Minh born; leaves Vietnam in 1911.
1914–1918	World War I.
1919	Ho tries to present a petition on behalf of Vietnamese independence at Versailles peace conference following end of World War I.
1925	Vietnamese Revolutionary Youth League founded in Canton, China.
1937	Japan invades China; first stage of conflict that will grow into World War II.
1940–1941	Japan takes over Vietnam. Ho Chi Minh returns to Vietnam and forms Viet Minh; begins resistance movement against Japanese.
1945	End of World War II. Ho Chi Minh declares Vietnamese independence and sets up government at Hanoi in north. French take control of Saigon and other areas in south.
1946	French attack northern Vietnam. War between French and Viet Minh begins.
1954	
May	Viet Minh defeat French at Dien Bien Phu.
July	Geneva Accords call for temporary division of Vietnam at 17th parallel, with elections to be held in 1956 to unify the country. Ngo Dinh Diem becomes premier of South Vietnam; Ho Chi Minh leads government in North Vietnam.
1955	United States sends advisers to train South Vietnamese army (ARVN). U.S. government backs Diem in refusing to hold promised national elections. Diem wins election in South Vietnam as "chief of state."
1956	Diem begins crackdown on those who resist his rule, calling them Viet Cong (Vietnamese Communists).
1960	Formation of National Liberation Front (NLF), political arm of the Viet Cong.
1961	President John F. Kennedy increases number of American military advis-

ers in South Vietnam from 900 to 3,200.

1963

May South Vietnamese troops fire on Buddhist celebration in Hue. Buddhist riots begin.

November Diem is killed in U.S.-backed coup by South Vietnamese military forces. Kennedy assassinated; Lyndon B. Johnson becomes U.S. President.

December American military advisers in South Vietnam total more than 16,000.

1964

August North Vietnamese PT boats reportedly fire on U.S. warships in Gulf of Tonkin. Congress passes Gulf of Tonkin Resolution, giving President unlimited power to resist aggression in Vietnam.

November Johnson reelected President.

1965

February Viet Cong attack Green Beret camp near Pleiku and army barracks near Saigon.

March U.S. begins Rolling Thunder bombing campaign of North Vietnam. U.S. Marines arrive at Da Nang—the first American combat troops in Vietnam.

April First antiwar march takes place in Washington, D.C.

July North Vietnamese Army (NVA) begins sending its own forces into South Vietnam to support Viet Cong.

August Marines defeat Viet Cong in Battle of Chu Lai.

October David J. Miller burns his draft card in protest against U.S. involvement in Vietnam.

October– U.S. Army defeats NVA in Battle of
November Ia Drang Valley.

December American soldiers in Vietnam total 184,000.

1966 U.S. sends 200,000 more troops to Vietnam. Senate Foreign Relations Committee hearings show that government officials are deeply divided over U.S. policy in Vietnam.

1967 U.S. sends 120,000 more troops to Vietnam, bringing total to about 500,000.

1968

January North Vietnamese attack marine base at Khe Sanh. Siege continues until April. Tet offensive begins. Viet Cong forces attack U.S. embassy compound in Saigon and cities and bases throughout South Vietnam. After bitter fighting, the offensive fails.

March President Johnson announces that he will not run for reelection.

August Democratic Convention opens in Chicago. Rioting and police violence are seen on television.

October Johnson ends Rolling Thunder bombing campaign.

November Richard Nixon wins presidential election, promising a "secret plan" to end the war.

1969

June Nixon announces Vietnamization policy. U.S. will gradually withdraw its troops and prepare South Vietnam's army to defend the country. U.S. troop level reaches peak of about 543,000.

September	Ho Chi Minh dies.		Defense Department report on origins of the war.
November	Largest antiwar demonstration takes place in Washington, D.C., drawing more than 500,000 Americans.	*December*	U.S. troop levels down to 159,000.
December	Number of American troops in Vietnam reduced to 479,000.	**1972**	
		October	Kissinger announces that secret negotiations have nearly brought about a cease-fire agreement. But South Vietnam's president objects to terms, and agreement is not signed.
1970			
February	Henry Kissinger and Le Duc Tho hold secret meeting to decide terms for U.S. withdrawal from war.		
April	Nixon announces U.S. incursion into Cambodia. Protests follow on many U.S. college campuses.	*November*	Nixon reelected President.
		December	Nixon orders heavy bombing of North Vietnam in order to force an agreement.
May	Ohio National Guard troops kill four students during antiwar demonstrations at Kent State University. Police kill two students at Jackson State College, Mississippi.		American combat troops are down to 24,000.
		1973	Paris Peace Accords (final cease-fire agreement) are signed, to go into effect January 28. Four Americans are killed in last five days of fighting.
December	Gulf of Tonkin Resolution repealed. American troop levels are down to 280,000.		
		1974	President Nixon resigns because of his role in the Watergate scandal.
1971			
February	South Vietnamese troops, supported by American airpower and artillery, invade Laos, but withdraw at end of March after meeting heavy resistance.	**1975**	
		March	North Vietnamese offensive against South begins with attack on Ban Me Thuot.
		April	Last Americans leave U.S. embassy in Saigon. South Vietnamese government surrenders.
June	*The New York Times* begins publication of Pentagon Papers, a secret		

The Wall

THE Vietnam Veterans Memorial in Washington, D.C., is almost never deserted. Day and night, in snow, rain, and sunshine, people go there to look for the dead. The short walk from the Lincoln Memorial takes you down a hill, and the sounds of the busy city are hushed. On your right is a flagpole and a statue of three soldiers. The soldiers, armed and draped with combat gear, appear to have halted to look at something in the distance. You follow their gaze and see the Wall, as the memorial is often called.

Made of black granite, the Wall begins at ground level and gradually rises. As you walk along the brick path beside it, you can read the names carved into its surface. The names make up a list of Americans who were killed in the Vietnam War. At the Wall's highest point, in the center, you must strain to make out the names at the top. Then the path slopes upward, leading you out of the memorial, and the Wall shrinks beside you, seeming to disappear into the earth again as the few final names appear.

The Wall is like the war. For Americans, the war began with the death of two military advisers in 1959. By the end of 1961, nine more names had been added to the list. Thirty more in 1962, and seventy-nine the year after that. As the United States sent its army, air force, and marines to Vietnam, the casualty lists rose like the Wall. In the peak year, 1968, more than 14,500 Americans died. After that, the troops began to come home. But the toll of the dead continued—until April 30, 1975, the very last day Americans remained in Vietnam, when four men were killed.

No one is buried at the Wall, but it contains the lost hopes and broken dreams of a generation of Americans. Those who visit it look for a part of their own lives, which were forever changed by the war.

Mothers and fathers, sons and daughters, wives and friends of the dead—all touch the names on the Wall, respecting, remembering, sorrowing. Some trace a name onto a sheet of paper so they can take a memory home. Children of those whose names are on the Wall come to remember the father they barely knew, and to tell him what he missed—and what they missed by growing up without him. Men who saw their buddies killed in the war come to weep and to speak their thoughts to the dead.

Visitors often leave something at the base of the Wall—poems, newspaper clippings, photographs, letters, childhood treasures and toys. They want to mark their loved one's sacrifice, or perhaps lay to rest a memory that haunts them still.

Many also come who were not yet born when the war ended and the last man died. Schoolchildren visit the Wall as part of their annual class trip. They too search for the name of someone—from their town, perhaps—who gave his life in Vietnam. They find the name, look at it for a while, and go away wondering why that person died. To most Americans, the reasons for the war are as unclear today as they were when the war was being fought.

Vietnam was the most unpopular war in American history. It was the war in which Americans marched in the streets to oppose their own government. It was the "bad war," the war we lost. And that makes the pain of those who fought it, and those who visit the Wall, that much greater. Nothing anyone can say today can end that pain, but we can try to understand what caused it.

This book will try to help you understand what happened, and why. Each of the more than 58,000 names on the Wall has its own story, known only to a few. So this is not the full story of Vietnam, or the only one that could be told. It is the larger story of Vietnam and the United States, and why so many people from both countries died. It starts long ago, in the past that shapes our lives today.

one

The Vietnamese and the French

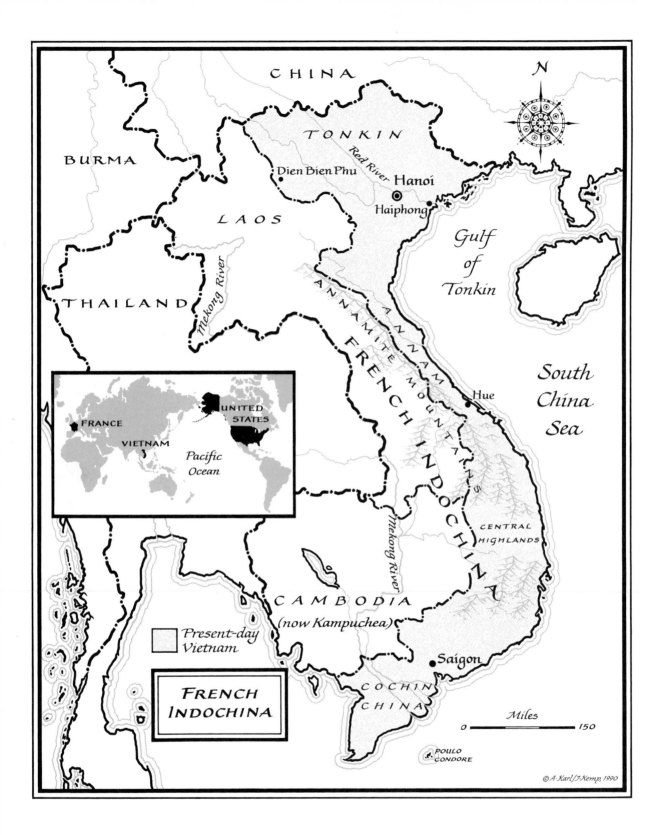

CHINA

N

TONKIN

Dien Bien Phu

Red River

Hanoi

Haiphong

LAOS

Gulf
of
Tonkin

BURMA

THAILAND

Mekong River

ANNAM

ANNAMITE MOUNTAINS

FRENCH INDOCHINA

South
China
Sea

Hue

CENTRAL
HIGHLANDS

FRANCE

UNITED
STATES

VIETNAM

Pacific
Ocean

CAMBODIA
(now Kampuchea)

Mekong River

Present-day
Vietnam

Saigon

FRENCH
INDOCHINA

COCHIN
CHINA

Miles

0   150

POULO
CONDORE

© A. Karl / J. Kemp, 1990

CHAPTER ONE

The Smaller Dragon

We have sometimes been weak and sometimes powerful, but at no time have we suffered from a lack of heroes.

—Vietnamese emperor Le Loi, 1428

THE Vietnamese people have a legend that five thousand years ago, they were ruled by a Dragon Lord—Lac Long Quang (pronounced Lack Long Kwahn). Lac was so able and good that his reign is remembered as a golden age. Lac married a beautiful fairy named Au Co (pronounced Ow Koe). Miraculously, she hatched one hundred sons from one hundred eggs. In time, the couple parted. Fifty sons went with their mother to the mountains. The other sons went with their father to the lowlands. The eldest son, Hong Bang, became the founder of the first dynasty, or ruling family, of Vietnam. He named his kingdom Au Lac after his parents. In their poetry, Vietnamese call themselves "the grandchildren of Lac."

The Vietnamese often called their country "the smaller dragon." The larger dragon was China, the country directly north of Vietnam. In Vietnam, the dragon is different from the one found in our familiar fairy tales. To us, the dragon is fierce, often a symbol of evil for a hero to slay. In Vietnam, the dragon was a water god, giver of life and food. The dragon stood for royalty, prosperity, and good luck. The throne of the emperor of Vietnam was known as the dragon throne.

Vietnam is located on the southeast corner of the Asian continent. It is shaped like a stretched-out *S,* more than 1,000 miles long—slightly smaller than California in size. To its west are the countries of Laos and Kampuchea (once called Cambodia). To the north is China, the world's

most populous nation. On the border with China and stretching west into Laos are beautiful blue misty mountains. The South China Sea washes against Vietnam's long coastline to the east and the south.

In ancient times the Vietnamese called their country Nam Viet, or "southern land." They lived in the area around the Red River, in the northern part of today's Vietnam. The Red River Valley was, and is, a fertile region, good for growing rice. In its journey to the sea, the Red River, called Mother River by the Vietnamese, deposits rich soil on the plains around it. For centuries, these plains were the heartland of Vietnam. The two major cities of this area today are Hanoi and Haiphong (pronounced High Fong).

Over a long time, the Vietnamese moved down the coast to the southern loop of the *S*—the Mekong River delta. The Vietnamese call it the River of the Nine Dragons because it splits into many streams before it reaches the South China Sea. The Mekong Delta is one of the most fertile rice-growing areas in Asia. Ho Chi Minh City (pronounced Hoe Chee Min), once called Saigon, is its major city.

The two river deltas of Vietnam, with their rich rice-growing lands, are often compared to two rice baskets on a carrying pole. The "pole" between the two deltas is a long narrow strip of land, in some places only

LEFT: *Two young women harvest part of their village's rice crop. One shoulders the "two baskets on a carrying pole" which the land of Vietnam has been compared to. The "pole" is a long, narrow strip that connects the fertile rice-growing regions of the north and south. (National Archives)*

RIGHT: *The Vietnamese had a talent for transforming the most ordinary materials. This child is wearing a raincoat made from bamboo leaves. (United Nations)*

twenty-five miles wide. In this strip, most people live close to the sea. To the west are grassy highlands and the Annamite Mountains, which are covered with dense jungles. This long mountain chain forms a natural border that prevented the Vietnamese from moving westward. Hue (pronounced Hway) is the major city of central Vietnam. The last Vietnamese emperors made this their capital.

Vietnam is a tropical country. Its most northern point is south of Florida. In the Mekong Delta, temperatures are often over 100 degrees, and the humidity is high as well. Northern Vietnam and the mountains to the west are cooler, but still the climate is warmer than in the United States.

The most important climate element is the yearly monsoon—a season when strong winds bring heavy rains. In the Mekong Delta, the monsoon season is from May to late November. Farther north, the monsoon comes between October and March.

The monsoon season sets the rhythm of life for the Vietnamese people, most of whom are farmers. This Vietnamese poem describes the work of a year's time:

> *The twelfth moon for potato growing,*
> *the first for beans, the second for eggplant.*
> *In the third, we break the land*
> *to plant rice in the fourth while the rains are strong.*
> *The man plows, the woman plants,*
> *and in the fifth: the harvest, and the gods are good—*
> *an acre yields five full baskets this year.*
> *I grind and pound the paddy, strew husks*
> *   to cover the manure,*
> *and feed the hogs with bran.*
> *Next year, if the land is extravagant,*
> *I shall pay the taxes for you.*
> *In plenty or in want, there will still be you and me,*
> *always the two of us.*
> *Isn't that better than always prospering, alone?*

For thousands of years, life in Vietnam has been a constant cycle of hard work. Rice, the major food, is grown in paddies, fields covered with shallow water. Unlike crops such as wheat or corn, rice plants have to be tended daily. Seedlings are taken up and replanted by hand. Weeding is a constant chore. When the rains come, the farmers must work together to build dikes to channel the water into the fields. In all these tasks, but especially in the careful management of the water supply, Vietnam's farmers have learned to cooperate to make the work easier.

The center of life in Vietnam was the village. Surrounding each village was a high bamboo fence separating it from the rice paddies. The fence bound together the people of the village, and at the same time separated the village from the rest of the world. Those within the fence formed a close-knit community of people working together for the good of all.

Each village was governed by its own members. They stored part of the rice harvest for use in times of famine and for distribution to the poor. Every village had a school where children learned to read and write. At the center of the village was the *dinh* (pronounced ding), a building which served as a meeting place and also housed the guardian spirit of the village. The Vietnamese believed that animals, plants, rocks, and water had spirits and personalities like humans, but were more powerful.

Family was all-important to the Vietnamese, and within each house lived several generations of grandparents, parents, and children. The family extended beyond the living as well. Vietnamese felt a close link with their ancestors and paid respect to them regularly. Inside each house was a tablelike shrine to these ancestors. The Vietnamese celebrated the anniversaries of their deaths much as we celebrate birthdays. On those days, a portion of food was set aside and placed on the ancestor's shrine. Children learned the names of their ancestors seven generations back—their great-great-great-great-great grandparents.

In times of peace, it was not unusual for Vietnamese to spend their whole lives in the area around their village. If a villager did leave to find work elsewhere, he was expected to return each year for the Tet holiday, Vietnam's New Year. No matter how far he traveled or how long he stayed away, the village was always his home. Every Vietnamese wanted to be buried in his home village, where he would be remembered and honored.

The Vietnamese, as "the smaller dragon," always faced the threat of the larger dragon to the north—China. In the third century B.C., the Chinese tried to make the Viets of the Red River region part of their empire. But as a Chinese record says:

> The Viets were extremely difficult to defeat. They did not come out to fight, but hid in their familiar mountains and used the jungle like a weapon. As a

Fireworks are exploded in the streets to drive away demons during Tet, the Vietnamese New Year. (Rene Burri/Magnum)

result, neither side could win. . . . The Viets would raid suddenly, rob, and get away fast, so that just as our army obtained its supplies from the home base, the Viets obtained theirs from our army.

This kind of hit-and-run fighting is known as guerrilla warfare. *Guerrilla* is a Spanish word meaning "little war." Over the centuries, the Vietnamese perfected their guerrilla tactics in the continual fight against China. It was the only way for an outnumbered people to resist a more powerful nation. More than two thousand years later, French and Americans would write military reports on Vietnam that were eerily like the Chinese report.

Despite the Viets' "little war" tactics, they were eventually overwhelmed by superior Chinese numbers and power. China brought Vietnam into its empire in 111 B.C.—about the time that Rome was building its empire in the West. For more than a thousand years, China ruled Vietnam. During this period, the Vietnamese adopted the Chinese systems of writing, education, and government.

The government system was based on the teachings of the Chinese scholar Confucius. Confucius taught that each member of society had certain duties toward the others. Society would operate well if every person carried out those duties. Within a family, for example, children should obey their parents. But the parents in turn had responsibilities to their children. The family was a mirror of the whole society. The emperor, like a parent, was the head of the nation. The people owed him certain duties, such as taxes. The emperor, for his part, was obligated to serve the people well.

The emperor's authority rested on the "mandate (or command) of heaven." If the emperor did not rule wisely, he could lose this mandate. Natural disasters, such as floods or earthquakes, were signs that heaven was displeased with the emperor. Such disasters, and the hardships they brought, sometimes caused the people to rise up in revolt. When a revolt was successful, its leader often became the new emperor. His success showed that he now had the mandate of heaven.

To administer his vast empire, the emperor used trained scholar-officials called mandarins. They carried the emperor's orders to the people, and so were treated with respect. In Vietnam, as in China, mandarins were chosen by an examination system. Confucian studies were among the subjects tested, but so were art and literature, for a mandarin was expected to be a cultured person. The examination system was open to all. In theory, even the child of the poorest farmer could become a mandarin if he studied hard. In reality, few farm children had the time to study, nor were their families able to afford a mandarin's education.

Buddhism also spread to Vietnam from China. Buddhism was a religion that began in India. Its founder was a rich young man who was troubled by the unhappiness he saw in the world. He gave up his wealth to search for the meaning of life. He is known to his followers as Buddha,

For centuries, trained scholar-officials called mandarins carried the emperor's orders to the people of Vietnam. The paddles held by the three mandarins in this 1917 photograph were badges of authority, as were their distinctive robes and hats. (The Bettmann Archive)

"the enlightened one." Buddhism urges people to accept hardship and sacrifice. Good actions would bring better things in the person's next life. A person would be reincarnated—born again and again—until he or she reached perfection, or enlightenment.

Though the Vietnamese adopted Buddhism and Confucianism, they kept their own spoken language, legends, and distinct cultural traits. Unlike the Chinese, they wore their hair long, painted their teeth, and tattooed their skin. The women of Vietnam were more independent than Chinese women. Although they could not be mandarins, Vietnamese women could own property.

During the long years of Chinese rule, the Vietnamese never lost a sense of themselves as a separate people. They longed for independence. In A.D. 40 two noblewomen, the Trung sisters (pronounced Troong), led a rebellion against the Chinese. Clad in golden armor and riding elephants, the Trung sisters led the Vietnamese to victory. But only two years later, the Chinese returned with a stronger force and put down the rebellion. Rather than surrender, the Trung sisters threw themselves into a river. Two centuries later, Trieu Au (pronounced Tree-yoo Ow), a Vietnamese Joan of Arc, fought the Chinese once again. When she was defeated, she too committed suicide.

Though these rebellions failed, the Vietnamese treasured the memories of the women who led them. Shrines in their honor could be found in the *dinhs* of small villages throughout the country. For centuries children have learned their names, and the names of other Vietnamese heroes who fought for independence. These names are as familiar in Vietnam as George Washington and Abraham Lincoln are in the United States.

In the tenth century, civil war divided China. The Vietnamese took advantage of the greater dragon's weakness to begin another revolt. The Chinese sent a fleet of ships to Vietnam to fight the rebels.

Ngo Quyen (pronounced No Kwen), another Vietnamese hero, prepared a trap for the Chinese. His men buried iron spikes in the bed of the Bach Dang River, where he knew the Chinese would land. At high tide, the spikes were hidden beneath the water. Ngo Quyen sent his own ships into the river. When the Chinese appeared, Ngo Quyen's ships retreated, drawing the Chinese forward. As the tide went out, Ngo Quyen's ships turned and attacked. They drove the Chinese fleet back onto the spikes, which now were above the water. The Chinese fleet was sunk, and the soldiers aboard were drowned. The Battle of the Bach Dang River in 938 is celebrated as the beginning of Vietnamese independence.

Forty years later China was again unified. To prevent another invasion, the ruler of Vietnam decided to send tribute, or gifts, to the Chinese emperor. Vietnam recognized China as its "protector." The official seal of Vietnam was brought to the Chinese court and kept there. The Chinese emperor's pride was satisfied, and for some time Vietnam would face no more invasions. It had its own emperor (who used the lesser title of "king" when writing to the Chinese emperor), and a separate system of government modeled after China's.

With independence, the fierce fighting spirit of the Vietnamese turned outward. They sought new lands because the Red River Valley was becoming overpopulated. Blocked to the north by China, to the east by the South China Sea, and to the west by the Annamite Mountains, they moved south. This gradual advance over more than eight hundred years was called Nam Tien, or the March to the South. In some ways, it was like the westward expansion of the United States. Villages sent out settlers who were helped by the mother village until they could support themselves.

To the south was the kingdom of Champa. It controlled the central part of today's Vietnam—"the carrying pole" between the rice baskets. The Vietnamese chipped away at Champa territory. In 1471, they won a major battle over the Chams and destroyed their capital. Many of the inhabitants were massacred. Some fled west to Cambodia and Laos, and others were absorbed into Vietnam.

The Vietnamese still had to fight to keep their independence. In the thirteenth century, the Mongols overran China. The Mongols were the fiercest fighters the world had ever seen. Led by Genghis Khan out of their small homeland north of China, the Mongols spread across the world as far west as Europe. They ruled China for nearly a century, and during this time they attempted to conquer Vietnam as well.

The Vietnamese general Tran Hung Dao (pronounced Tran Hun Dow) led the resistance to the Mongols. Vastly outnumbered, the Viets again used the tactics of guerrilla warfare. They avoided large battles and hid in the mountains, coming out only to stage surprise attacks against the Mongols. Three times the Mongols captured Hanoi, the Vietnamese capital, and each time they were forced to leave. General Dao repeated the trick of burying spikes in the Bach Dang River that Ngo Quyen had used 350 years before. Finally, the Mongols gave up. The fight for Vietnam was not worth the cost.

Vietnam's struggles were not over. In 1407, a new Chinese dynasty sent its powerful army south and regained control of the country. The Chinese outlawed such customs as tattooing and wearing long hair. But another in Vietnam's long line of heroes arose—Le Loi (pronounced Lay Loy). Calling himself "the pacifying prince," he swore to free his country. Like the legendary English King Arthur, he had a magic sword. Le Loi had received his from a turtle in a lake. Once more, the Vietnamese used guerrilla warfare to defeat the forces of "the greater dragon." Le Loi established a new dynasty, the Le. He called his capital Dong Kinh, from which comes Tonkin, the name for northern Vietnam.

In the sixteenth century, the strength of the Le dynasty declined. Vietnam was split between two powerful families. The Trinh family (pronounced Trin) seized control in the north, the Nguyen family (pronounced Noo-yen) in the south. Both families recognized the Le emperor, but he was just a figurehead with no real power. When the Trinhs tried to win control of the south, the Nguyens kept them out by building a wall across the narrow center of Vietnam.

The Nguyens continued the march to the south. In the eighteenth and nineteenth centuries, they pushed out the Cambodians who lived in the Mekong Delta. The Cambodians never forgot this, and their hatred of the Vietnamese still lives.

The Vietnamese had reached their second rice basket. They found life in the Mekong Delta easier than in the north. The soil was richer and the problem of flooding was less severe. Many southern Vietnamese intermarried with the people who had lived there earlier. Southerners came to be regarded as more easygoing than the northern Vietnamese. The tradition of resistance was not as strong in the south because the south had not been part of the country at the time of Chinese domination.

In 1773, about the time of the American Revolution, a rebellion against the Nguyens broke out in the south. It was led by three brothers from the village of Tay Son (pronounced Tie Shun). The Tay Sons won support by taking land from the rich and giving it to the poor. High taxes and rents had made the Nguyen family unpopular among the peasant farmers, and the rebellion was successful. Then the Tay Son brothers marched north, where they were welcomed by the peasants.

The Chinese used this revolt to try to regain the Viet kingdom. This time the Viet hero was Nguyen Hue (pronounced Noo-yen Hway), one of the Tay Son brothers. He chose to attack during the Tet holiday, which comes at the same time as the Chinese New Year (usually February). As the Chinese were celebrating, Nguyen Hue's forces, mounted on elephants, struck. The Chinese were caught off guard and were driven back to a bridge across the Red River. Their commander was among the first to flee across the bridge. When his forces followed in panic, the bridge collapsed, drowning many and leaving the rest at the mercy of Nguyen Hue's men. That was in 1788. One hundred and eighty years later, another "Tet offensive" would have an equally spectacular effect on U.S. forces.

During the time Vietnam was divided between the Trinhs and the Nguyens, a new force had entered the country—Europeans. All over the Far East in the sixteenth century, Portuguese traders arrived on caravels, strong sailing ships like the ones Christopher Columbus had used to cross the Atlantic. The Portuguese—and later, other Europeans—set up small trading posts to exchange their goods for the spices and other products of the East. Soon they were followed by Christian missionaries.

The most influential missions in Vietnam were established by the French. The missionaries won many Vietnamese converts. Alexandre de Rhodes, a French priest, perfected a system of writing Vietnamese with the Roman alphabet, the letters we use in English. This system is still used today. Having to learn only twenty-six letters—instead of the thousands of Chinese characters that were previously used—made it much easier for people to learn to read and write.

The missionaries became involved in Vietnamese politics. After the Tay Son brothers died, there was no strong ruler to take their place. French missionaries saw this as an opportunity to increase their influence in Vietnam. One member of the Nguyen family had escaped the Tay Sons. With military support from France, he reestablished control over the country in 1802. He took the name Gia Long (pronounced Ya Long) and became the first in a new line of Vietnamese emperors—the Nguyens.

Gia Long called his country Vietnam, or "southern land." He set up his capital at Hue, in the "carrying pole," and his dynasty would last until 1955. For most of that time, however, the French were the real rulers of Vietnam.

By accepting French military help, Gia Long had opened the door to further French influence in Vietnam. Though France was a strong Catholic country, its interest in Vietnam went beyond winning converts. Around the world, Europeans were setting up colonies—European settlements that were controlled by the home nation. European countries received great economic benefits from their colonies. They took the natural resources of the country and sold their own manufactured products there. France saw Vietnam as a potential prize in the European race to build colonies in Asia.

French missionaries tried to change the customs of the Vietnamese,

Two women and a young boy at prayer in a church built by Christian missionaries. Efforts to convert Vietnamese to Catholicism led to French political control over the country. (Werner Bischof/Magnum)

such as ancestor worship. In turn, the mandarins grew uneasy at the missionaries' increasing power. They persuaded Gia Long's successors to drive out the French and outlaw Christianity. When some missionaries were executed, the French government sent a military force to protect the others. Soon the French would go farther.

Superior technology and weapons of war had helped Europeans to overcome people in America, Africa, and Asia. So it was in Vietnam as well. In 1859, the French attacked Saigon. Like the Chinese invaders in the past, they did not find victory easy. "As long as grass grows on our soil, there will be men to resist the invaders!" a captured rebel in the Mekong Delta cried out as he faced a French firing squad. Before long the French had to send reinforcements.

Because the Vietnamese emperor was occupied with a rebellion, he decided to give up Saigon and the provinces around it in 1863. But France was not satisfied. Ten years later, it sent troops to attack northern Vietnam. In 1874, the French forced Vietnam's emperor to sign the Treaty of Hue. It allowed the emperor to keep his throne, but French colonial officials controlled the government.

The Vietnamese turned to China for help, but China had its hands full fighting European attempts to establish colonies on its soil. In 1884, China turned over to the French the Imperial Seal of Vietnam, the sign of China's "protection" over Vietnam. In a public ceremony in Hue, the French consul shattered the seal to show that the French had replaced the Chinese. France was now Vietnam's "protector," and it ruled more harshly, and more directly, than the Chinese had.

Vietnam was divided into three parts—Tonkin in the north, Annam in the central region, and Cochin China in the south. Along with Cambodia and Laos, which France had also conquered, Vietnam became part of what was called French Indochina.

Though the name Vietnam disappeared from the map, the Vietnamese did not forget their identity. All over the country, shrines to the Trung sisters, Trieu Au, Ngo Quyen, Tran Hung Dao, Le Loi, and other Vietnamese heroes reminded the people of their ages-long struggle for independence. Rebellions continued to bedevil the French for years.

The Vietnamese had defeated the powerful forces of the Chinese and the Mongols. They were determined to fight off this new conquerer as well. A wall poster of the late nineteenth century threatened: "If you persist in bringing to us your iron and flame, the struggle will be long. But we are guided by the laws of Heaven, and our cause will triumph in the end."

CHAPTER TWO

The Book of the Wise

There is a legend, in our country as well as in China, on the miraculous "Book of the Wise." When facing great difficulties, one opens it and finds a way out.

—Ho Chi Minh, 1960

IN their colonial system, the French had two conflicting goals. On the one hand, they saw their role as a civilizing mission. They believed that French culture was superior to the cultures of the colonized peoples. Therefore, the French could best serve these "backward" people by civilizing them—that is, making them as much like the French as possible. With time (and it might be a long time), the people of the colonies would become like "little brothers" of the French.

Opposed to this goal was the more immediate need for profit. The French stripped Vietnam of timber, coal, and other natural resources. They gave themselves a monopoly on such products as alcohol, opium, and salt. As the only legal source of these products, they could charge whatever they wanted. For the Vietnamese, the salt monopoly was a particular hardship. Before refrigerators, in a country without ice, salt was needed to preserve food.

The French set up large plantations, where they grew rubber trees, coffee, tea, and rice. Using Vietnamese laborers, they built canals, roads, bridges, and railroads throughout the country. They beautified and improved Saigon, which became known as the Paris of the Orient. In Tonkin, the north, the French built textile factories and coal mines.

But ordinary Vietnamese received little benefit from these improvements. Profits from the plantations, the factories, and the mines went directly to France. Much of Vietnam's rice crop was exported to other countries, so within Vietnam the price of rice rose, and there was less for each person.

To pay for the modernization of Vietnam, France made large loans to the colonial government. The government in turn taxed the people of

French colonials sitting on the terrace of the Grand Hotel in Saigon show how luxurious life in the colony could be. The waiters, of course, were Vietnamese. (Roger-Viollet)

Vietnam to pay back the loans. Villagers who could not pay their taxes lost their land—land that their ancestors had farmed for generations. They went to work as tenant farmers for rich landlords. Some, desperately poor, took jobs as laborers in the rubber plantations and coal mines. Special agents signed up laborers for a three-year period. The pay was poor and the conditions dangerous, but workers who tried to leave before the three years expired were fined or jailed.

Vietnamese known as culture brokers worked for the French government in much the same way as the emperor's mandarins had. Their chief qualification was that they could speak both languages, and thus could carry French orders to the Vietnamese. They often used their positions to enrich themselves. When the French closed the village schools and gave money to the culture brokers to set up new ones, many brokers kept the money instead. The result was a sharp drop in education for most Vietnamese.

Vietnamese rebellions continued during the twentieth century, but the

French, with their superior weapons, put them down with great brutality. Rebel leaders were beheaded, tortured, or sent to the feared French prison island of Poulo Condore off the coast of southern Vietnam.

The French tried to stamp out any sense of Vietnamese nationalistic pride. Even the name Vietnam was outlawed. Though the emperor kept his court in the city of Hue, he was totally dominated by the governor-general of French Indochina, who ruled in Hanoi. As Confucians would have said, the emperor no longer had the "mandate of heaven" that gave him the authority to lead the people.

What the Vietnamese needed most was a goal, an ideal that could command the respect the emperor once held. Some looked for that ideal to the Chinese revolution, which had overthrown the last emperor of China in 1911. Others visited Japan, which had armed itself with modern weapons to become the strongest military power in the Far East. Some studied European ideas. They were in search of a Book of the Wise—a legendary book that Vietnamese turned to for advice when they were in trouble. This time the book would tell them how to free their country once more from

Vietnamese digging and carrying coal at a French-owned mine. The French claimed to be helping Vietnam by developing its mineral resources, but the Vietnamese never saw any of the profits. (United Nations)

THE EDUCATION OF A REVOLUTIONARY

The most privileged Vietnamese attended school with the children of the French colonists. Truong Nhu Tang (pronounced Troon Nyew Tahn), a student at one such school in Saigon, described his experiences there:

> We spoke and wrote [only] French, and we learned, along with the mathematics, science, and literature, all about the history and culture of *nos ancêtres les Gaulois* ["our ancestors the Gauls"—the people who lived in France two thousand years ago]. We learned by heart the geography of France; we knew her literature, her people, her art. We read of France's great political and military heroes, her men of science and of letters. We felt at home in the great worldwide civilization that these illustrious "ancestors" of ours had created. About our own country we remained profoundly ignorant, except for what we read in the final chapters of our history books, the ones on France's colonial empire, France *outre-mer* ["overseas"]. But our ignorance did not disturb us; in fact, we were not even aware of it. It wasn't until after I had begun secondary school that I began to realize that I was—in some ways at least—different.
>
> The scene of my initiation into the mysteries of colonialism was the . . . schoolyard during recess. As the games we played became rougher and more competitive, my Vietnamese friends and I learned that we, in contrast to our French schoolmates, were part of a racial entity sometimes called *nhaques* [peasants], sometimes *mites* [an insulting form of "Annamite," the French term for Vietnamese]. . . . I was first shocked by the insults. Soon shock gave way to anger, and recesses were occasionally punctuated with brawls, which mirrored the hatreds felt by many of our elders. . . . As I began to feel the first stirrings of my Vietnamese identity, [I was not] in the least aware of how the French had come to master Vietnam or of the history of Vietnam's dealings with previous masters.

a foreign invader. The person who would find that message, and carry it back to Vietnam, was the greatest Vietnamese leader of the twentieth century—Ho Chi Minh.

Ho Chi Minh was not his real name. It was only the most famous of the many names he used in his life. For many years he roamed the world, working as a revolutionary. Yet his burning desire always was to bring about the independence of his homeland. In spite of his long absence, he became a famous figure in Vietnam, and many Vietnamese looked to him for leadership.

In later years, when the world knew him as Ho Chi Minh, a reporter asked him to clear up the questions about his life. Ho smilingly refused, saying, "An old man likes to have an air of mystery about himself. I like to hold on to my little mysteries."

One thing was sure—those who met him were always impressed. Many were caught and held by his dark, penetrating eyes. A Vietnamese student who met him in 1946 noted "an air of fragility," but added that Ho sent out "a combination of inner strength and personal generosity that struck me with something like a physical blow. He looked directly at me . . . with a magnetic expression of intensity and warmth." His fragility masked a steely interior that never swerved from its purpose. To children, he was kindly "Uncle Ho"; to his enemies, he was a ruthless opponent.

Ho was born Nguyen Sinh Cung (pronounced Noo-yen Shin Koon)

The young emperor Bao Dai (middle, beneath fans) appears outside his palace in Hue around 1930 with the French "resident" (right)— an official representative of the French government. The emperor was in fact only a "puppet" of France's colonial officials. (Roger-Viollet)

in 1890 in Nghe An province (pronounced Nay Ahn) in northern Annam, in what later became North Vietnam. His home was a long straw hut in a traditional village. As a boy, he fished and played near the rice paddies and bamboo groves that surrounded the village. Occasionally he went to Hue, where his father served as a mandarin in the emperor's court, a position Ho's father once described as "the ultimate form of slavery."

Rebels against French rule were active in Nghe An province, and Ho's family supported them. At one point, their home was a hiding place for workers who had deserted a French road-building project. Ho's older sister worked in a French military camp and stole arms and ammunition for the rebels. She was caught and sent to prison. (Years later, in 1945, she saw a photograph of Vietnam's new head of state. Thinking he resembled her long-lost brother, she traveled to Hanoi with a gift of eggs and geese from the family farm. Despite their years of separation, brother and sister recognized each other and embraced.)

Ho attended a French secondary school in Hue. He clashed with his schoolmaster, a former French soldier who bullied his students. Leaving without receiving a diploma, Ho went south and taught in a village school for a short while. Then he was off to Saigon—the only time he was known to have been in the city that today bears his name. In 1911, at the age of twenty-one, Ho left Vietnam. He would not return to his homeland for thirty years.

For about three years, Ho was a kitchen worker on a French cargo ship. He reached the United States, where he saw Boston and San Francisco before settling in New York, taking jobs as a laborer. Like a tourist, he was impressed by the city's skyscrapers. But more important to him was the fact that Chinese immigrants lived in their own section of the city, with the full rights of American citizens. He saw that Americans put their ideals of freedom and democracy into practice. After about a year in the United States, Ho went to England. There he worked in the plush Carleton Hotel as a pastry cook under a famous French chef named Escoffier.

By this time, World War I had broken out in Europe. France and England were fighting Germany in bloody trench warfare. During the war, more than 100,000 Vietnamese were brought to France as soldiers and laborers. Ho left England for Paris, the capital of France, where he would remain for six years. He had talent as an artist, and took a job painting vases that were sold as Chinese "antiques." Soon he became a photo retoucher. He advertised his services in a French newspaper, using the name Nguyen Ai Quoc (pronounced Noo-yen Eye Kwook), which means Nguyen the Patriot.

Ho was inspired by Paris, with its monuments to French heroes and the ideals of the French Revolution, whose eighteenth-century leaders had overthrown the king. Inscribed on many public buildings was the motto of the Revolution: *liberté, egalité, fraternité*—liberty, equality, fraternity. He found the city still alive with exciting talk of politics and human rights. He went to political meetings and distributed leaflets describing "the crimes committed by the French colonialists in Vietnam."

Ho found sympathetic and eager listeners, but he was confused by the many new ideas they offered him as the correct path to follow. He wandered the streets of Paris and sat on the banks of the Seine River to read the books and pamphlets people had given him. He was searching for his Book of the Wise.

In 1917, the United States entered World War I on the side of France and England. Less than a year later, U.S. President Woodrow Wilson presented the Fourteen Points, his program for peace. Among Wilson's points was a promise of "self-determination for subject peoples"—people who were ruled by other nations, larger and stronger than their own.

Ho understood Wilson's promise to mean that the people in European colonies would be allowed to choose their own form of government. He felt that Wilson would help the Vietnamese recover their independence.

After Germany's defeat in 1918, the leaders of the winning nations gathered at the Palace of Versailles just outside Paris. Filled with idealism, Ho traveled to Versailles. He tried to present a petition to President Wilson on behalf of the people of Vietnam. "All subject peoples," the petition read, "are filled with hope by the [promise] of right and justice."

Ho never got to see Wilson. The leaders of the peace conference had no time for such unimportant, unknown people as Nguyen the Patriot. But in Vietnam, newspapers reported Ho's effort and printed his words and his picture. The Vietnamese people knew that someone had stood up to demand their freedom. The name Nguyen Ai Quoc became a rallying cry for those who still struggled against the French.

Disappointed by Wilson's rejection, Ho turned elsewhere. During the war, revolution in Russia had overturned the country's monarchy. Vladimir Lenin took power and set up the Soviet Union, the world's first Communist government. Lenin was inspired by Karl Marx, a German philosopher who had predicted that workers would overthrow their rulers and set up a society without social classes—a system that was called communism. After the Communist revolution, Marx thought, all people would be equal. There would no longer be rich or poor.

Ho had been to Marxist meetings in Paris. Now he sought out Lenin's books and began to read them. He found them difficult, but he forced himself to read them again and again. He read of Lenin's support for the freedom of colonial peoples. These were words that promised to free his people from the French. Sitting alone in his small room, Ho felt tears come to his eyes. He shouted aloud, imagining himself addressing great crowds: "This is what we need. This is the path to our liberation." Ho had found his Book of the Wise, and devoted the rest of his life to bringing it to the people of Vietnam.

In 1924, Ho went to the Soviet Union. He joined the Communist International, or Comintern, an organization that promoted Communist revolutions throughout the world. The Comintern trained him to organize others to work for the revolution. During the 1920s and 1930s, Ho followed the orders of the Comintern, working to spread communism in many countries of Asia. But his mind was always on Vietnam.

Another revolution would bring Ho a step closer to Vietnam. In 1911, Nationalist rebels overthrew the last emperor of China. Two thousand years of Chinese history were swept aside.

Sun Yat-sen, the leader of the Chinese Nationalist party, wanted to unify and modernize China. But warlord bandits controlled large parts of the country. Sun asked for help from the Soviet Union, China's neighbor. Soviet instructors went to Sun's headquarters in the city of Canton to help train his army, which included both Communists and Nationalists.

In 1925, the Comintern sent Ho Chi Minh to Canton. Many Vietnamese were already living there, after fleeing French rule in their homeland. They hoped to learn how to apply the lessons of the Chinese Revolution to Vietnam. Ho brought some of these people together to form the Vietnamese Revolutionary Youth League.

Members of the Youth League received military training and learned how to persuade others to join their cause. Some of the Youth League's members then returned to Vietnam and organized demonstrations against French rule and strikes in the mines and rubber plantations. League members taught other Vietnamese about communism and made new recruits. Their organization worked like a chain letter, in which each new member's job was to spread the movement to others.

Slowly the league grew stronger. By the end of 1929, it had more than one thousand members. One of them was twenty-year-old Pham Van Dong (pronounced Fam Van Dong), who would one day be the premier of Vietnam. Dong's father was an important mandarin in Hue. His son developed an intense pride in his country and an equally intense hatred for the French. As a teenager, Dong had led students through the streets with banners telling the French to get out. The French arrested him, and when he got out of jail, he fled to Canton, where he met Ho.

Ho was impressed by Dong's zeal and skill. The two formed a close personal bond. Ho called Dong "my best nephew," and their friendship lasted until Ho's death.

In 1927, China ceased to be a safe place for Communists. Sun Yat-sen had died, and his successor, Chiang Kai-shek (pronounced Chang Kie-sheck), turned against his Communist allies—both Chinese and Soviet. He hunted down Chinese Communists and killed them. Ho left China and returned to the Soviet Union.

His movements during the next few years are not clearly known. He appeared in Thailand, disguised as a monk and living in a Buddhist monastery. He recruited more Communists among the Vietnamese living there. In 1930 he was in Hong Kong, a British colony off China's coast, where he helped to found the Indochina Communist party.

Though Ho had not been in Vietnam since 1911, the French feared him enough to condemn him to death if and when he was caught. When British police in Hong Kong arrested Ho in 1931, the French asked that he be sent back to Vietnam. But somehow Ho kept from falling into French hands by arranging a report of his own death. The last entry in the Hanoi police file on Nguyen Ai Quoc was: "Died in Hong Kong prison, 1933."

Ho, of course, was alive. For unknown reasons, he was released from prison in Hong Kong in 1933. Once again, his life story contains a gap. He would not reappear in China until 1938. A year earlier, Japan had invaded China. To gain allies against the Japanese, the Nationalist leader Chiang Kai-shek patched up his differences with the Chinese Communists. Once more Ho was able to use China as a base of operations.

In 1940, Pham Van Dong rejoined Ho in China. Dong brought with him the third member of the trio that would make a revolution in Vietnam—Vo Nguyen Giap (pronounced Voe Noo-yen Yahp). Giap, born in 1910, was to become the military genius behind the Vietnamese revolution. Giap had gone to a French school in Vietnam, where he had been a brilliant student. Later he taught history in a high school.

Giap's students never forgot his passion for the French Revolution and for France's great general Napoleon. One of them recalled Giap prowling the floor of the classroom, "possessed by the demons of revolution and battle" as he described each of Napoleon's campaigns. Giap knew every detail by heart. Back and forth he paced, describing the battles so clearly that his students felt they were witnessing them as they took place.

The teacher of history would soon have the opportunity to make history himself. He knew the stories of Vietnam's military heroes as well, and how they had fought for their country's independence. One of his heroes was Nguyen Ai Quoc. For years, Giap had carried with him a newspaper clipping with the photograph of the young man who had tried to present Vietnam's case at the Versailles peace conference. Now, twenty-one years later, Giap met the patriot for the first time. As Giap recalled:

> A man of mature years stepped towards us wearing European clothes and a soft felt hat. Compared with the famous photograph . . . he looked livelier, more alert. He had let his beard grow. I found myself confronted by a man of shining simplicity. This was the first time I had set eyes upon him, yet we were already conscious of deep bonds of friendship.

Together, Pham Van Dong, Vo Nguyen Giap, and Ho Chi Minh would lead the Vietnamese to victory over two of the world's most powerful nations.

The Japanese invasion of China was the first stage of the conflict that grew into World War II. In 1940, Japan's European allies, the German Nazis, swept into France. After France surrendered, the Japanese moved into the French colony of Vietnam. The French administrators were allowed to remain, but the Japanese held the real power in the country.

Many Vietnamese cooperated with the Japanese, preferring them to the French. But Ho wanted no foreign rulers for Vietnam—he urged his followers to oppose both the French and the Japanese. He finally returned to Vietnam in 1941, after thirty years away, and set up his headquarters in a cave near the Chinese border.

Here, in May 1941, around a bamboo table with only blocks of wood to sit on, Ho, Dong, Giap, and several others formed the League of Independence of Vietnam—called the Viet Minh. Its purpose was to unite

Japanese troops patrol Saigon on bicycles during World War II. The Japanese said they were liberating their Asian brothers from the European colonialists, but they were as ruthless as the French had been in governing Vietnam. (AP/Wide World)

Vietnam's people in a single struggle for independence. Ho insisted that all patriotic Vietnamese should be welcome within the Viet Minh—Communists, non-Communists, Buddhists, Catholics, farmers, city dwellers, even landlords.

From a small radio station, Ho spoke to his people. "More than twenty million sons and daughters of Lac [the mythical ancient Dragon Lord of Vietnam] are determined to do away with slavery," he said. "Now the opportunity has come. . . . Let us unite together! . . . Victory to Vietnam's revolution!"

The Viet Minh soon attracted followers. Though Ho's northern base was far from any major city, his party's control spread in an ever-widening area.

Sometime during the war, Ho discarded the name Nguyen Ai Quoc and took the name by which he would be known in history: Ho Chi Minh, "Ho who enlightens." It had a special meaning for the majority of Vietnamese, who were Buddhists. One who was enlightened had reached the highest stage of life. By taking this name, Ho claimed to be the true leader of the Vietnamese people.

In daring to oppose the Japanese, Ho had gambled that he would attract Japan's enemies to his side. His chances improved in December 1941 when the Japanese bombing of Pearl Harbor in Hawaii brought the United States into World War II. During the war, members of Ho's Viet Minh rescued American pilots who were shot down in Indochina. They also passed information about Japanese troop movements to the U.S. Office of Strategic Services (OSS). The OSS sent Americans behind enemy lines to train, equip, and fight with those forces opposed to the Japanese.

In 1945, OSS advisers flew from a base in China and parachuted into an area near Ho's headquarters. Soon they were brought to his hut. A French intelligence report had prepared them for a man who was "cunning, fearless, sly, clever, powerful, deceptive, ruthless—and deadly." Instead they found what they described as "a pile of bones covered with yellow dry skin." Ho had malaria, and the OSS members treated him with medicine from their kits.

The French, nervous about American cooperation with the Viet Minh,

This picture of Vo Nguyen Giap (left) and Ho Chi Minh was taken when OSS advisers from the United States visited Ho's headquarters during World War II. (AP/Wide World)

had insisted that a French officer, disguised in an American uniform, accompany the OSS mission. After Ho recovered, he sat down at a meeting with the Americans. He startled everyone when he began by pointing to the Frenchman. In the English he had learned on the streets of New York, the fragile-looking Asian gentleman said, "Look, who are you guys trying to kid? This man is not part of the deal." The French officer was sent back to China.

The OSS advisers stayed with Ho's forces, sharing their diet of rice and bamboo shoots. Giap asked them for weapons, and soon U.S. planes were dropping rifles, machine guns, grenades, and small mortars. The OSS held training classes for some of the Viet Minh troops and found them quick and eager to learn.

According to one American who talked with Ho Chi Minh during the war, Ho "knew American history well and he would talk about American ideals and how he was sure America would be on his side. . . . He thought that the United States would help in throwing out the French in establishing an independent country."

The President of the United States, Franklin Delano Roosevelt, did in fact disapprove of French rule in Indochina. He told an aide, "France has had this country . . . for nearly one hundred years and the people are worse off than they were in the beginning."

But Roosevelt's primary goal was victory in World War II. He needed the support of the Free French troops, led by General Charles de Gaulle. The importance of France in the postwar world had to be considered. Any plans Roosevelt might have had for Vietnam ended when he died in April 1945.

A month before Roosevelt's death, the Japanese in Vietnam jailed the remaining French administrators and their troops. Bao Dai (pronounced Bow Die), the Vietnamese emperor who had docilely served the French, now shifted his loyalty to the Japanese. At their urging, he declared Vietnam independent from France, but Japan's troops still occupied the country.

In July 1945, the new U.S. President, Harry S Truman, met with his allies, the leaders of the Soviet Union and Great Britain. Germany was already defeated, and victory over Japan was only a matter of time. The allies discussed what to do with the territories now occupied by Japan. In regard to Vietnam, they agreed that when the Japanese surrendered, Chinese troops would move into the northern part of the country. In the south, a British force would be sent to accept the surrender of the Japanese. No decision was made on the postwar status of Vietnam.

On August 6, 1945, the United States dropped an atomic bomb on Hiroshima, Japan—the first ever used in warfare. As news of the awesome destructive power of the bomb spread, it became clear that Japan would soon surrender. The end of World War II was near. In Vietnam, Ho Chi Minh moved swiftly to establish his own control before the French could return.

Presenting themselves as allies of the United States, the Viet Minh moved into the cities. The Japanese knew they were finished—they did not resist as the Viet Minh flag was raised over public buildings. Bao Dai, the puppet emperor who had served both France and Japan, gave up his throne and turned over his seals of office to the Viet Minh. To Vietnamese, this was a significant event—the "mandate of heaven" had passed to Ho Chi Minh.

On September 2, Ho went to Hanoi to declare the independence of Vietnam. Before a cheering crowd in the city's main square, he began his speech with his own version of words from the American Declaration of Independence (supplied by an OSS officer): "We hold the truth that all men are created equal, that they are endowed by their Creator with certain unalienable rights, among them life, liberty, and the pursuit of happiness." American planes flew overhead in a display of friendship, and a Vietnamese band struggled through "The Star-Spangled Banner."

Throughout the city and the country as far away as Saigon, the Vietnamese celebrated. At last they were free of foreign rule. Bao Dai, now "supreme counselor" to Ho's government, wrote to General Charles de Gaulle. Bao Dai told De Gaulle of the joyous and determined mood of the country . . . and gave him a warning at the same time:

> You would understand better if you could see what is happening here. . . . Should you re-establish a French administration here, it will not be obeyed. Every village will be a nest of resistance, each former [friend] an enemy, and your officials and colonists will themselves seek to leave this atmosphere, which will choke them.

Alas, General de Gaulle did not heed the advice.

CHAPTER THREE

The Elephant and the Tiger

It will be a war between an elephant and a tiger. If the tiger ever stands still, the elephant will crush him with his mighty tusks. But the tiger will not stand still. . . . He will leap upon the back of the elephant, tearing huge chunks from his side, and then he will leap back into the dark jungle. And slowly the elephant will bleed to death. That will be the war of Indochina.

—Ho Chi Minh, 1946

THE French had no intention of giving up Vietnam. France's pride had been deeply wounded by its surrender to the Germans in the early years of World War II. It wanted to regain its former glory as a great world power with a large empire.

Ho Chi Minh hoped that his wartime help to the United States would give him a powerful supporter. But the agreement President Truman had made—to let the British take the Japanese surrender in the southern half of Vietnam—would eventually bring the French back.

General Douglas Gracey was the commander of the British troops sent to Saigon to take the surrender. He sympathized with the French. When the Viet Minh leaders asked him if they could set up a government in the south, as they had in the north, Gracey refused.

Without a formal government, there was chaos in the city. To bolster his small force, Gracey freed the French soldiers who had been imprisoned by the Japanese. On September 22, 1945, French troops raised their country's flag over Saigon's public buildings. The French residents of the city, who had stayed indoors to avoid attack, now rampaged through the streets. They insulted and attacked the Vietnamese while French and British soldiers stood by and did nothing.

Two days later, the Vietnamese launched a general strike. Vietnamese workers stayed at home, and the city ground to a halt. Streetcars stopped running, and shops and markets were closed. That night people cowered behind locked doors, listening to the sounds of explosions and gunfire in the streets. Vietnamese crippled Saigon's electric power plant and broke into French homes, killing more than 150 people, including women and children.

In early October, troops from France arrived in Vietnam. The French commander, General Jacques Leclerc, confidently declared that the country would be pacified within four weeks. But the Vietnamese blew up bridges, mined roads, and ambushed French soldiers at night. The war between the elephant and the tiger had begun.

In the north, where Chinese troops had moved in to take the Japanese surrender, the Viet Minh government was firmly in place. Ho Chi Minh had made sure there would be no rivals to his leadership by wiping out any opposition. However, famine threatened the country. During the war, the Japanese had taken rice from Vietnam to feed their troops. Now, heavy rains caused flooding that could ruin the rice crop.

Ho appealed to the age-old Vietnamese spirit of cooperation. Thousands of people worked to repair damaged dikes to stop the flooding. Ho declared that vacant land could be claimed by anyone willing to farm it. People planted quick-growing crops such as potatoes and manioc roots. In every village, wall posters spread the slogans "Not one square foot of uncultivated land" and "Not a single man idle." The efforts succeeded, and by the spring of 1946, most people had enough to eat. By his actions, Ho had shown his ability to lead the country.

Ho faced another problem—how to get rid of the Chinese troops that still occupied much of the north. Chinese soldiers were looting homes and terrorizing the people. Ho feared that the Chinese would resume their ancient domination of Vietnam. To get the Chinese out, he agreed to discuss a new relationship with France. He felt that in the long run the Chinese were a greater threat than the French.

In March 1946, the Viet Minh and the French reached a temporary agreement. At the end of May, Ho sailed to France for what he thought would be the signing of a formal treaty.

But the French in Vietnam pressured the French government not to give in to Ho. General Charles de Gaulle—whose role in World War II had won him the respect of his country—argued that without its empire, France would become a second-rate power. Ho spent the summer of 1946

in France, arguing his case for independence. But in the end the French refused his demands.

Ho sailed back to Vietnam, knowing that he had failed. By the time he returned in October, the French were already preparing to reoccupy northern Vietnam by force.

In November, French troops attacked Haiphong, a port city on the coast near Hanoi. From the harbor a French ship fired artillery shells into the city's streets. French fighter planes dropped bombs and fired on frightened crowds. Six thousand people were killed. The French grew confident. "If these gooks want a fight, they'll get it," the French commander bragged as he came ashore in Haiphong.

The French demanded that all Viet Minh in Hanoi give up their weapons. In response, the Viet Minh attacked French neighborhoods and military posts. The next day French soldiers swept into the city. By the time they reached Ho Chi Minh's house, he had escaped. The tiger was loose, and for the next eight years he would give the elephant no peace.

Ho and his government retreated into the countryside. From there, Ho called to the Vietnamese by radio:

> Men, women, children, old or young . . . if you are Vietnamese, rise up to fight the French colonialists to save our country. He who has a gun, let him fight with a gun; he who has a sword, let him fight with a sword; he who has neither gun nor sword, let him fight with spears, with pickaxes, with sticks. Let no one stay behind.

Ho's call inspired the Vietnamese people. At last, they had a leader they could rally around.

Most of the large battles of the war for independence would take place in the north, but the Viet Minh had supporters in the south as well. Fifteen-year-old Xuan Vu (pronounced Soon Voo), who lived in a Mekong Delta village in the south, wrote:

> My village and all the other villages . . . belonged to the Viet Minh, heart and soul. Everyone was part of the movement, everyone supported it. . . . We had been slaves of the Chinese for a thousand years, slaves of the French for a hundred. Now we were going to be free. The feeling was everywhere. . . . It was unstoppable.

The Viet Minh sent organizers throughout the country to win new recruits for their cause. By 1947, General Giap claimed the Viet Minh had more than a million members. Most were ordinary people who did whatever they could to fight the French. They planted booby traps and bombs; they sheltered and supplied the Viet Minh's fighting forces. Xuan Vu became a recruiter for the Viet Minh:

> We'd go into a village and just walk around . . . telling them to come to our meeting. . . . We'd start off with some patriotic songs. . . . We'd talk about the fact that there were no schools [and say] "Look, you can't read, you can't write. You are ignorant. Do you know why? . . . because of the French. . . . They've kept you like animals—do you like that?" . . . Then we'd go around with a sign-up list, for people . . . to join the Youth League. They'd all join. . . . They knew that the chances of their actually becoming real fighters wasn't very good. . . . But at least they could . . . pay their ten cents dues every month and be part of what was going on.

With this network of support, Giap's fighters could go anywhere in the country and find places to eat and sleep. The French might control the cities—although there too the Viet Minh planted bombs—but the country-side belonged to the Viet Minh. Throughout the country the French tried to establish strong points by building small military camps with fortified watchtowers. But when their troops left the camps to go on patrol, the Vietnamese were waiting in ambush. True to Ho's call, they used whatever weapons they could steal from the French or make themselves.

They dug small pits with sharpened bamboo "punji sticks" at the bottom. The pits, covered with branches or grass, were deadly traps for any French soldier who stepped on them. Vietnamese who had no rifles used bows and arrows, homemade crossbows, and poisoned darts.

The French tried to win Vietnamese support by turning to the former emperor, Bao Dai. He had left the Viet Minh government and was leading a life of pleasure in Hong Kong. The French lured him back with promises of greater freedom for Vietnam. In 1949, the French restored him to the throne and made Vietnam an "associated state" within the French Union. But French officials still made the important decisions.

Women as well as men answered Ho's call to chase the French out of Vietnam. They planted booby traps, sheltered the Viet Minh's fighting forces, and, like this woman, took their turn at guard duty. (Library of Congress)

Bao Dai's "puppet government" claimed to rule all of Vietnam, both north and south. To support him, the French trained loyal Vietnamese to form a national army. But Bao Dai's army was never strong enough to hold the country without French soldiers. Every day, the Viet Minh reminded France that Vietnam still had heroes who wanted freedom.

For Americans, the French war in Indochina might have remained an unimportant struggle in a faraway land. But in the years after World War II, Americans became concerned about the growing power of the Soviet Union. After the war, the Soviets took control of eastern Europe, installing Communist governments in Hungary, Poland, Czechoslovakia, and other nations. Communist rebels threatened Greece and China as well. Americans feared that these moves were part of a Soviet plan to spread communism all over the world.

The French played on Americans' fear of communism. They portrayed their struggle in Vietnam as a fight against communism, rather than a fight to dominate the Vietnamese.

Ho Chi Minh sent letters to President Truman, asking for help in his battle against the French. Truman gave him the same response President Wilson had in 1919—he never answered the letters. OSS members who had met with Ho insisted that he was primarily a nationalist—a Vietnamese patriot. But to Truman and his advisers, what was more important was that Ho was a Communist. To them, this meant he took his orders directly from Moscow, the capital of the Soviet Union. And though the Soviets had been America's allies in World War II, the United States now saw them as a threat. Despite Ho's claims of friendship with the United States, the American government regarded him as part of the "worldwide Communist conspiracy."

America's attitude toward communism hardened when the Chinese Communists won their long civil war with the Chinese Nationalists in 1949. Communist leader Mao Zedong (pronounced Mow Zee-dong) named the new government the People's Republic of China. Though President Truman had sent aid to the Nationalists during the civil war, some Americans accused his administration of having "lost" China. The world's most populous nation was now under the red flag of communism. It seemed to many Americans as if a "red tide" were sweeping over the world.

The People's Republic of China sent weapons to the Viet Minh, and

THE ANTI-COMMUNIST WITCH-HUNT

Many politicians have built careers by warning Americans of Communist "subversion"—secret attempts to weaken the United States. But one particular senator, Joseph R. McCarthy of Wisconsin, went far beyond the rest in making reckless accusations of disloyalty. In fact, the word *McCarthyism* was coined to mean the making of any wild, unproved charge. However, for a time McCarthy so dominated American politics that almost no one had the courage to oppose him. His cry of "Communist!" made even presidents cower, and in the process ruined the lives of many Americans.

McCarthy shot into the spotlight in 1950, when he waved a sheet of paper while speaking before an audience in Wheeling, West Virginia. He claimed it was a list of Communists in the State Department. The number of Communists on his list varied from speech to speech—and McCarthy never disclosed the actual names. But he fooled many Americans into believing that he was sincere in his anti-Communist "witch hunt."

McCarthy was head of a Senate committee at the time. He dragged numerous people before the committee and grilled them about their alleged Communist sympathies. People had to account for statements they had made many years before. McCarthy investigated charges sent in by people who suspected their neighbors or co-workers of Communist leanings.

Throughout the early 1950s, McCarthy's hunt for disloyal Americans spread into all areas of American life. Many people were fired from their jobs because McCarthy or others branded them as Communists. Government workers, university professors, and people who worked in the entertainment industry were among those placed on "blacklists," keeping them from getting jobs. Those in the State Department who had advised cooperation with Communists during World War II— when Soviet Russia was our ally—were dismissed. Thus, only ardent anti-Communists were left to determine U.S. policy in such countries as Vietnam.

McCarthy lost his hold on the American public after he charged that there were Communists within the U.S. Army. Televised hearings gave Americans a firsthand look at McCarthy's method of smearing others with the charge of disloyalty. Most Americans didn't like what they saw, and McCarthy's popularity ebbed. His Senate colleagues, who had earlier tolerated him, voted to condemn him.

Though McCarthy's power faded, the fears he had raised remained strong. Future American leaders felt they had to take action against any Communist movement anywhere in the world. No one wanted to be accused of being "soft on communism." No one wanted to face the charge of "Who Lost China?" that had dogged President Truman. The main reason why American presidents of the 1950s, 1960s, and 1970s sent military aid to South Vietnam was that they did not want to face the question, "Who lost Vietnam?"

at the beginning of 1950, China became the first foreign nation to recognize the Viet Minh as the legal government of Vietnam. The Soviet Union soon followed. United States Secretary of State Dean Acheson's response was sharp: This "should remove any illusions as to the 'nationalist' nature of Ho Chi Minh's aims and reveals Ho in his true colors as the mortal enemy of native independence in Indochina." To Acheson, Ho was not a Vietnamese patriot, because he was a Communist and accepted help from Communist nations.

Most Vietnamese would not have agreed. Ho's followers included many non-Communists who supported him as the leader of the anti-French forces. Many Vietnamese regarded those who supported the French as traitors. So, when the United States recognized the French-backed Bao Dai government in early 1950, it put itself on the side of the colonialists rather than the freedom fighters. It was the first step that led the United States into its war with Vietnam.

Another Asian war brought American troops into the region. In June 1950, Communist North Korea suddenly invaded South Korea. The United States sent military forces to support the South. Non-Communist members of the United Nations joined the effort to repel North Korea's attack.

When the fighting moved close to the Chinese border, the People's Republic of China entered the war on the side of North Korea. Though a truce ended the war in 1953, the United States was more determined than ever to stop Communist aggression anywhere.

The United States stepped up its aid to the French forces in Vietnam. In 1950, President Truman had sent a few military advisers to show French soldiers how to use American weapons. Although these advisers were not used in combat, they were the first U.S. soldiers in Vietnam.

When President Eisenhower took office in 1953, he increased U.S. aid to the French in Vietnam. France was eager to shift the burden of the war onto someone else, and by 1954 the United States was paying close to 80 percent of the cost of the war. Even so, Eisenhower carefully avoided sending any U.S. fighting troops.

At home, France was war-weary from eight long years of fighting. By mid-1953 the French had lost 74,000 soldiers in Vietnam. Another 190,000 were still fighting there. Many French citizens had lost faith in what some called "the dirty war."

In May 1953 a new French commander arrived in Vietnam—General Henri Navarre. He believed that he could defeat the Viet Minh by luring them into a major battle. Then the superior resources of the French would wipe them out. As the site for his trap, Navarre picked a remote village on the northwest border with Laos—Dien Bien Phu.

French commander Christian de Castries surveys the hills surrounding his camp at Dien Bien Phu, 1953. De Castries hoped to lure the Viet Minh into a major battle there and then wipe them out. He and his superiors seriously misjudged the Viet Minh's ability to place soldiers and artillery in those hills. (National Archives)

Dien Bien Phu (pronounced Dee-en Bee-en Foo) was at the center of communications and transportation between China, Laos, and Vietnam. But it was isolated from the main French forces in the country. Navarre deliberately placed a sizable group of French troops there to draw the Viet Minh into attacking. He predicted victory in words that would haunt the Vietnam War for years: "Now we can see it clearly—like light at the end of a tunnel."

In November 1953, French paratroopers landed at Dien Bien Phu. Major Marcel Bigeard told his paratroopers, "You're going where men go to die." Because of the remote location, all supplies had to be flown in, so the French immediately began to build airstrips. A ring of fortresses was established around the base. In these, the French placed artillery that they believed would chop up an attacking force. The French destroyed forests around the base so that the Viet Minh would have no place to hide. If they attacked, they would have to come across open ground.

However, Dien Bien Phu was surrounded by high hills. An enemy who could bring artillery to these hills to bombard the base below would have a tremendous advantage. But the French believed that General Giap's troops could not possibly move heavy artillery through the rugged terrain and up the hills. Even if they did manage to bring up a few guns, French airpower (provided in part by Americans) would knock them out.

As they had before—and would again—the Vietnamese surprised their enemies with their determination. The Viet Minh troops took apart their artillery guns and carried them piece by piece through the jungle, on bicycles and on their backs. By March 1954 the Viet Minh had more than two hundred large guns on the hills overlooking Dien Bien Phu. In the valley, the French had only forty guns of similar size. By the time the French discovered their mistake it was too late.

The French also misjudged the number of troops Giap could bring to the battle. Now in his early forties, Giap personally led the forces gathering around Dien Bien Phu. By radio, he summoned his people from all over the north. In the Viet Minh army, soldiers trained, worked, and fought in teams of three. The teams stayed together and watched out for each other for as long as they remained soldiers. To reach Dien Bien Phu, they marched for twelve hours a day, with ten minutes rest each hour. Each man carried a thirty-pound bundle of rice, a shovel, a water bottle, and salt in a bamboo tube. Wearing sandals made of tires, the soldiers sang as they marched along paths through the mountains and jungles. By early March, Giap had 50,000 men around Dien Bien Phu, against 13,000 French inside.

When Colonel Christian de Castries, the French commander in the camp, learned of the Viet Minh's strength, he considered pulling his troops out. But his artillery chief assured De Castries that his guns would take care of the Vietnamese. When Giap realized the French would not try to escape, he cheered. "They are staying. This time I have them."

On March 13, the carefully hidden Vietnamese artillery guns roared, and shells rained down on the French positions. Viet Minh troops charged and overran two of the three French artillery posts in the first two days of fighting. The French airstrip was also knocked out, and any further supplies had to be dropped by parachute. The French artillery chief who had reassured De Castries committed suicide.

The problem of supply became desperate for the French. When American and French pilots flew into the area, the Viet Minh shot them down with brand-new antiaircraft guns from China. The Viet Minh hid their artillery in caves and under trees. The planes sent to destroy them could not find the targets. Supply planes faced devastating fire.

The monsoon rains arrived, covering the area with heavy clouds. Now Dien Bien Phu could receive no more supplies by plane. The defenders were cut off from the outside world. They dug their trenches deeper into the mud as the Viet Minh artillery continued to bombard Dien Bien Phu.

Giap set his men to work building trenches and tunnels, closer and closer to the camp. The French had cut down forests so the Viet Minh could not hide in them—but now the enemy was coming underground. At night, the Viet Minh set up loudspeakers that blared their message to the French: "Surrender or die!"

These women are carrying ammunition to the Viet Minh troops in the hills around Dien Bien Phu. (Library of Congress)

Relentless pounding by Viet Minh artillery drove the French soldiers out of their barracks and into narrow, cramped trenches. (The Bettmann Archive)

As the situation grew worse, France asked the United States for more help. President Eisenhower's military experience made him unwilling to join a fight that was already lost. Some of his advisers argued in favor of using atomic bombs. But Eisenhower avoided action by saying that the United States would act only if it was joined by Great Britain. As Eisenhower knew, the British were unwilling.

However, Eisenhower was concerned about the effects of a Communist victory. At a press conference, he said, "The loss of Indochina will cause the fall of Southeast Asia like a set of dominoes." This idea, called the domino theory, was later used to justify direct American involvement in Vietnam.

After the Viet Minh destroyed the airstrip at Dien Bien Phu, all supplies and reinforcements had to be dropped by parachute. (AP/Wide World)

FRENCH INDOCHINA VETS

There was one woman among the French at Dien Bien Phu. She was Genevieve de Galard, a nurse who worked at the underground hospital. A month before the battle ended, the camp celebrated her twenty-ninth birthday. Colonel De Castries, the French commander, gave her the Legion of Honor, France's highest military medal. When the Viet Minh overran the camp, she was among those taken prisoner, but was soon released.

The other French prisoners were treated harshly. Many did not survive the brutal conditions of their captivity. One who did later said:

It was all for nothing. I let my men die for nothing. In prison camp the Viets told us they had won because they were fighting for an ideal and we were not. I told them about my paras [paratroopers] at Dienbienphu. I told them how they fought. And they said, "Heroism is no answer."

Like later American veterans of Vietnam, French soldiers were not greeted with parades on their return home. They had fought in a war that divided France. Some branded them as brutal; others called them failures for having lost the war. Many veterans had trouble finding jobs; some felt comfortable only with others who had served in Indochina.

One French vet recalled his homecoming: "We were considered pariahs [outcasts], criminals. Three days after I came home I was wearing my uniform because that was all I had to wear. I got on a bus. When I passed in front of the driver he said to the ticket taker, 'Hey, an assassin just got on.' I hit him and spent the rest of the day at the police station."

Even so, the French vets remained proud of their service to France. "We are happy to have suffered together," said one vet. "There was in the army at that time a spirit that no longer exists. One was involved."

At Dien Bien Phu, the French grew desperate. Their base had originally been four miles wide by twelve miles long. By the first week of May, they held an area only as large as a baseball stadium. The base had an underground hospital, but there were only forty beds. More than 6,000 men had been wounded. Men lay unburied where they died. Ammunition and food were practically gone.

De Castries told his men, "I expect all the troops to die . . . rather than retreat an inch." And, true to his word, he did not surrender. When the Viet Minh broke into his command post, he radioed orders for the artillery to shell it. But the artillery was silent—it had been overrun as well. On May 7, the Viet Minh raised their flag over the command bunker. De Castries, along with more than 10,000 other men, was taken prisoner.

At Dien Bien Phu, General Giap must have felt he had gained the victory that would finally bring Vietnam its independence. But soldiers can only win battles; diplomats decide who wins the war. Far away, in Geneva, Switzerland, the diplomats had already gathered to determine the future of Vietnam.

Great Britain and the Soviet Union had called the Geneva Conference to discuss the problems of both Korea and Indochina. American, French, and Chinese representatives were also at the conference. As scheduled, the delegates took up the question of Indochina on May 8. When the diplomats met that morning, all were aware that Dien Bien Phu had fallen the day before.

Vietnam sent two delegations to the conference. One was headed by Pham Van Dong, who represented the Viet Minh. The other represented Bao Dai's government, which was backed by the United States. Both Bao

Viet Minh parade in victory through the streets of Hanoi, northern Vietnam, in 1954. The French had been defeated at last. (AP/Wide World)

Dai and Ho Chi Minh claimed to rule all of Vietnam. By supporting Bao Dai, the United States hoped to salvage something from the French defeat.

All over Vietnam, people knew that the heroes of the Viet Minh had dealt a final blow to the French. Pham Van Dong insisted that the Viet Minh's military victory gave them the right to rule the country. He expected the Soviet Union and Communist China to support him.

But the two large Communist powers wanted peace. The Chinese had suffered terrible losses in the Korean War. They were now interested in winning friends among other Asian nations. As for the Soviet Union, its longtime leader, Joseph Stalin, had died the year before. His successors were trying to work out a more peaceful relationship with the United States and other western nations. Neither of Ho's Communist allies was willing to fight in Vietnam to support him.

Thus, the Soviets and the Chinese pressured Pham Van Dong to agree to a compromise. A dividing line was drawn between northern and southern Vietnam at the 17th parallel. Bao Dai's government would control the area south of that line. The Viet Minh would rule in the north.

The French troops would withdraw from the north, but could temporarily remain in the south. The Viet Minh soldiers in the south would leave and go north. For a 300-day period, civilians could move to either side of the line.

The 17th parallel was specifically defined as *not* being a permanent border. Vietnam was granted its independence, and the French would eventually leave. To unify the country, national elections would be held two years later, in 1956. (The neighboring countries of Cambodia and Laos, which had been part of French Indochina, were also given their independence.)

These agreements were part of what was called the Geneva Accords. Although the United States did not sign the accords, it said it would not block them. It would soon break that promise.

two
The United States in Vietnam

CHAPTER FOUR

The First Steps into the Tunnel

*Diem is the best hope that we have in South Vietnam.
. . . He deserves and must have the wholehearted
support of the American government.*

—U.S. Senator Hubert Humphrey, 1956

*Diem is a bad choice. . . . Without him, some solu-
tion might be possible, but with him there is none.*

—French Prime Minister Edgar Faure, 1956

WHILE the Geneva Conference was being held, the United States was already moving to make sure communism would not spread south of the 17th parallel. It sent aid and advisers to Bao Dai, now ruling in Saigon, the great city of the Mekong Delta area. Bao Dai, having served the French, the Japanese, the Viet Minh, and again the French, was not an inspiring figure. He was used to having others do the work of governing for him. Before the Geneva Conference was over, Bao Dai announced that Ngo Dinh Diem (pronounced No Din Yee-em) was now the premier of his government.

Diem, then fifty-three, appeared to be what the United States wanted—a non-Communist Vietnamese patriot who could challenge Ho Chi Minh's popularity among the people of Vietnam. Diem's father—like Ho's—had been a mandarin in the emperor's court in Hue. But Diem's family—unlike Ho's—was Catholic and had grown wealthy during the French colonial days. However, Diem opposed French control over his country. He shared Ho Chi Minh's goal of an independent Vietnam, yet he and Ho were bitter enemies.

The split between the two men dated from World War II. When the Japanese took over the country, Diem's older brother Khoi worked for them. The Japanese tried to wipe out the leadership of the Viet Minh, and

September 1954. At the port of Haiphong in northern Vietnam, refugees crowd the deck of LST-901, a U.S. ship that will take them south. Many are Catholics who hope that life will be better for them under the government of newly appointed Catholic leader Ngo Dinh Diem. (National Archives)

Khoi, himself an anti-Communist, cooperated in the effort. The Viet Minh captured him and buried him alive.

Still, when Ho formed his government in 1946, he offered an important post to Diem. Ho wanted to broaden his support by including both Communists and non-Communists in the government. But in a face-to-face meeting, Diem called Ho a criminal and refused to take any role in the Viet Minh government. Four years later, in 1950, as the Viet Minh began to win their struggle against the French, Diem heard that Ho had put his name on an assassination list. Fearing for his life, Diem fled to the country.

After a stay in Europe, Diem came to the United States and lived in a Catholic monastery near New York City, reading and praying. In his youth, he had considered becoming a priest and never married. On occasional trips to New York City, he made important political friends—including the young Catholic Senator John F. Kennedy. When the news came that Bao Dai had appointed Diem to head his government, Diem's friends felt that Diem would provide strong leadership for the anti-Communist Vietnam they wanted.

Unfortunately, they misjudged his character. When he flew back to Vietnam, crowds of people gathered along the road to the airport, waiting to catch a look at their new premier. Diem rode by them in a chauffeured limousine with curtains covering the back windows. He didn't look out, and no one on the road saw him. That was the way he would rule Vietnam—like a mandarin of old, or, as some said, like a Confucian emperor. He was a remote figure, surrounded by armed guards. He alone decided what was good for Vietnam and what was not. He trusted few people outside his own family. As one of his relatives once said, "He comes from another planet."

As agreed at Geneva, the last French troops left the northern part of Vietnam in October 1954. The Viet Minh took over the north, with Ho Chi Minh as president. South of the 17th parallel truce line, the French were slower in leaving. While they delayed, President Eisenhower began to send U.S. military advisers to replace French officers in training Bao Dai's army. The United States was ready to take over the role the French had played—at least in the south.

Eisenhower's secretary of state, John Foster Dulles, was determined to stop the spread of communism at the 17th parallel. Though both Bao Dai and Ho Chi Minh still claimed that Vietnam was one country, the Americans began to refer to the two halves as "North Vietnam" and "South Vietnam." Dulles felt that the Americans could build up South Vietnam as a bulwark against Ho Chi Minh's Communist forces. Because the United States was not interested in colonies, it could succeed where the French had failed. No one could accuse the United States of trying to rule Vietnam. South Vietnam was, officially, our newest ally in the Far East.

American hopes rested on the shoulders of Ngo Dinh Diem. Among his problems was that he was a Catholic leader of a mostly Buddhist country. However, he tried to increase his supporters by encouraging North Vietnam's Catholics to come south during the three hundred days when people could move freely to either side of the 17th parallel. He was helped by the American Central Intelligence Agency (CIA), which had replaced the OSS as the U.S. agency in charge of spying and secret operations. CIA airplanes dropped leaflets in the North, telling the people that "Christ is going South." By boat and by land, about 900,000 people, mostly Catholic, left North Vietnam and moved to the South.

A much smaller number of Vietnamese went north—around 100,000. Most of these were members of the Viet Minh. They were following the agreement made at Geneva that required them to regroup in the north. These "regroupees" expected that the elections promised for 1956 would unify the country, and they could then return to their homes in the South.

Eisenhower sent a CIA officer, Colonel Edward Lansdale, to advise Diem. Lansdale had played a key role in the Philippines, helping its newly independent government defeat Communist guerrillas. The Americans hoped Lansdale could duplicate this success in Vietnam.

Lansdale won Diem's confidence and became one of the few outsiders Diem trusted. The first task Diem faced was to strengthen his control over all parts of the South. There were several powerful groups that threatened him. Though these groups were non-Communist, they had their own small armies and virtually ruled parts of the country. Encouraged by Lansdale, Diem sent his army to destroy or disarm them one by one. To the Americans, Diem looked like the winner they needed.

Lansdale worked behind the scenes as well. Many Vietnamese believed in the predictions of astrologers, who foretold the future by studying the stars. Lansdale slipped money to some of these astrologers to ensure good predictions for Diem and bad ones for Ho.

Since 1954, the North Vietnamese had been trying to get Diem to discuss plans for the nationwide elections that would unify the country. The elections would clearly ask Vietnamese to choose between Diem and Ho. But in June of 1955, Diem announced that no elections would take place. Secretary Dulles publicly backed Diem's decision.

Years later, President Eisenhower admitted that the United States could not allow the elections to be held because Ho Chi Minh would have won. It proved to be a tragic decision. If the United States had not backed Diem at this time, Vietnamese voters might have settled their nation's future without the massive bloodshed that followed.

On Lansdale's advice, Diem held his own election in May 1955, among the people of South Vietnam. He asked them to choose between himself and Bao Dai as the ruler of the country. Bao Dai had returned to the good life in Paris. But in theory, he had the power to replace Diem. With him out of the way, Diem's power would be unchallenged.

Lansdale cautioned Diem against rigging the election. As Lansdale wrote later, "I said, all you need is a fairly large majority. I had to go to Washington . . . and I said, 'While I'm away I don't want to suddenly read that you have won by 99.99 per cent. I would know that it's rigged then.'" So Diem played it safe—he won with 98 percent of the votes. Few thought the election was an honest one, but only the Communists protested.

Diem was now in complete control of the government in Saigon. However, as Lansdale tried to make him realize, that was not enough. It was one thing to control the government, but another to control the people—as Diem never did.

What every Vietnamese farmer most wanted was to have his own plot of land. Diem could have helped these farmers—and won their support as well—when his government took control of plantations that had been abandoned by French owners. But instead of giving the land to the farmers, Diem offered it for sale. Most of it went to wealthy Vietnamese, increasing the gap between rich and poor.

When the Viet Minh had controlled part of the South, they had given land for free to the Vietnamese who farmed it. Diem took back this land and gave some of it to Catholics who had moved from the North after the Geneva Accords. Diem's policies made many people long for the return of the Viet Minh.

Diem also tried to increase his control over the country by appointing new village chiefs—a policy that went against centuries of tradition. In earlier days the saying was, "The emperor's rule stops at the village gate." Even the French had allowed the villagers to elect their own chiefs. Worse yet, the new village chiefs were chosen only for their loyalty to Diem. And like the corrupt culture brokers during the French years, many enriched themselves by pocketing American money intended to help the villagers.

Lansdale wanted Diem to go into the countryside like an American politician, to meet his people and find out what their concerns were. In 1957, on one such trip, Diem was shot at by a discontented villager. From then on, he stayed within areas where his troops could protect him. Even at large, carefully organized political rallies in Saigon, the citizens who gathered to cheer Diem were kept well away from the man who ruled them.

Diem's trips to the countryside were carefully staged affairs. Here, surrounded by guards and advisers, he presents a bicycle to an old woman. (François Sully/Black Star)

More and more, Diem stayed within the presidential palace. Everyone knew when he ventured forth, because his limousine would speed through the streets surrounded by police cars, their sirens wailing. Suspicious of everyone except his own relatives, he put his brother Ngo Dinh Nhu (pronounced No Din Nyew) in charge of a secret police force that hunted down anyone who opposed his rule.

There was only one remaining source of opposition to Diem—the Viet Minh. Many Viet Minh in the South had chosen not to move north. Instead, they had returned to their villages and put away the weapons they had used against the French. Now, Diem's policies caused many of them to take up arms again. Former Viet Minh members began to assassinate the village leaders who had been appointed by Diem. They also killed or kidnapped teachers and technicians that the government had sent to the villages.

The Viet Minh was not a completely Communist organization. Many had joined its ranks only because they wanted to free their country from French rule. Diem might have won their support. Instead, he began to crack down on anyone who had fought with the Viet Minh against the French. His secret police jailed and killed many suspects, including those who only spoke out against Diem. The prison island of Poulo Condore, where the French had tortured Vietnamese patriots, quickly filled with people whom Diem distrusted.

Diem began to call all of his opponents Communists, or "Viet Cong." The name was meant to be an insult, but it became a rallying cry among the villagers. Few Vietnamese peasants understood communism fully. They knew only that the Viet Cong opposed Diem. Those who suffered from Diem's policies, or wanted their own plot of land to farm, now began to think of themselves as Viet Cong.

The ranks of the Viet Cong (VC) grew larger when the Viet Minh members who had gone north—the regroupees—began to slip back into the South, with Ho Chi Minh's blessing. They could not come directly across the 17th parallel, which divided the country, because around that line there was a demilitarized zone (DMZ) where no armed troops were allowed to enter. So, beginning in March 1959, the regroupees left North Vietnam and walked down a network of trails in Laos, on the eastern border of Vietnam. This route became known as the Ho Chi Minh Trail.

WALKING THE HO CHI MINH TRAIL

The high, jungle-covered mountains along the border between Vietnam and Laos are lonely, forbidding places. In ancient times, people used elephants to thread their way through the passes between the mountains. During the war with the French, the Viet Minh moved from north to south along primitive paths in this region, where French troops rarely patrolled. After the fighting stopped in 1954, jungle growth quickly covered the paths.

In 1959, North Vietnam's leaders decided to help the Viet Cong who were fighting Diem's regime. Because the DMZ formed a barrier between North and South, supplies and soldiers would have to go through the mountains, and the trails had to be cleared again. The job of reopening them was given to a team of southerners led by an old man who knew the way. The path they cut was called "the old man's trail" at first, but as the war went on it became known as the Ho Chi Minh Trail.

In the early 1960s, the trail was still nothing but a system of camouflaged footpaths that wound through rugged mountains 7,000 feet high. The main trail went south through Cambodia and into the Mekong Delta west of Saigon, and parts of it branched off into South Vietnam. Stations along the way provided food, clothing, medical care, and guides to lead groups to the next station. One of those who took the trip early in the war recalled, "Road? It is not even a path, just a simple track opened by our guides in the low brush on the sides of the mountain, sometimes only crude steps cut into the bare rock."

The first soldiers to use the trail were re-groupees—former Viet Minh who had gone to the North after the Geneva Accords. Each soldier had to carry an eighty-pound pack that contained everything he would need to live and to fight—an extra uniform, two pairs of sandals, raincoat, nylon tent, hammock, mosquito netting, rope, food, and medicine. Marching up to twelve miles a day, many soldiers collapsed from the heat and humidity; others, weak from dysentery caused by drinking unclean water, fell by the wayside. Tigers and leopards stalked the jungles, but there was no time to stop for anyone who could not keep up the pace. By one account, only about half the men and women who started down the trail made it through.

As the war expanded, so did the trail. Tens of thousands of workers gradually widened the paths, paving them with crushed rock so that trucks could bring supplies from the North. American B-52s constantly bombed the trail after 1965, but work crews quickly built bypasses around sections that had been destroyed. Large villages grew up around the original way stations, with warehouses, fuel stations, hospitals, and even farms. The Ho Chi Minh Trail became the artery that supplied troops and weaponry to the Communist forces fighting in the South. Because it went though neutral countries—Laos and Cambodia—American troops could not cross the border to attack it. (For a map of the Ho Chi Minh Trail, see page 70.)

The Viet Cong's strength grew rapidly. Between mid-1959 and mid-1960, the VC killed around 2,500 government officials in the countryside. Roads outside the cities became unsafe, and soon the Viet Cong grew bold enough to attack military outposts. In July 1959, six of them crept into the airbase at Bien Hoa (pronounced Bee-en Hwah), only twenty miles north of Saigon. Two American military advisers, Sergeant Chester Ovnand and Major Dale Buis, were killed while they were watching a movie. Their names are the first ones on the Vietnam Veterans Memorial in Washington, D.C.

In the villages, the Viet Cong carried on the work of winning converts to their side. Diem had paved the way for them. The Viet Cong promised the villagers land and the right to choose their own leaders. By the end of 1960, the government had lost the support of much of the countryside. In the daytime, Diem's army enforced his authority. But at night his troops returned to their bases, and the Viet Cong came forth and organized the villagers against Diem, the same way the Viet Minh had done against the French.

In December 1960, with support from Ho's government in Hanoi, a group of Viet Cong members met to set up the National Liberation Front (NLF). The NLF was to be the political organization of the Viet Cong—setting policies that were transmitted to Viet Cong throughout the South. The NLF declared its determination "to free the country from *My Diem*" (pronounced Me Yee-em; meaning America/Diem). Its flag, half red and half blue with a gold star in the middle, stood for "the two halves of the nation, united under the star—in a single purpose."

Viet Minh regroupees follow a jungle path at night, headed south to reinforce those who oppose Diem's rule. The guerrillas carry small torches made from perfume bottles and leaves. (Eastfoto)

CHAPTER FIVE

Two Deaths in November

Let every nation know, whether it wishes us well or
ill, that we shall pay any price, bear any burden, meet
any hardship, support any friend, oppose any foe to
assure the survival and the success of liberty.

—John F. Kennedy,
  inaugural address, 1961

THE problem of Vietnam was turned over to a new American President when John F. Kennedy took office in 1961. The youngest man ever elected President, Kennedy represented a new generation of leadership. Handsome and vigorous, he said during his campaign that he wanted "to get the country moving again." In his inaugural speech, he challenged the idealism of young Americans by declaring that the United States would "bear any burden" in the cause of freedom.

"Ask not what your country can do for you," Kennedy said. "Ask what you can do for your country." Kennedy's words inspired many Americans with a new sense of pride and purpose. They were ready and willing to go wherever Kennedy might lead them.

Kennedy had long been interested in Vietnam. As a senator, he had visited the country in 1951. The first Catholic to be President, Kennedy admired his fellow-Catholic Diem for his anti-Communist fervor, which Kennedy also shared.

Kennedy felt the United States could halt the spread of communism with a new military approach. Communist rebels, or insurgents, won by using guerrilla tactics and by organizing the people. Kennedy and his advisers developed the idea of counterinsurgency. Militarily, the insurgents could be beaten by arming and training people at the village level to defend their homes. At the same time, political and social reforms would give the people reasons to support their government. American aid pro-

THE GREEN BERETS

President Kennedy found that the spirit and tactics of the U.S. Army's Special Forces matched his ideas of what counterinsurgency should be. The Special Forces—nicknamed the Green Berets for their distinctive headgear—had been formed in 1952. Their purpose was to organize anti-Communist guerrilla forces. Their work was often secret, and they sometimes carried out CIA-planned missions.

Some Special Forces units had been operating in South Vietnam since 1957. Their chief mission was to organize the primitive tribes who lived in the Annamite Mountains between Vietnam and Laos. The French called these people *montagnards*—"mountain people." The Vietnamese themselves thought of them as *moi*—savages, not really Vietnamese. But the Green Berets found the montagnards useful. They were good fighters and helped to prevent the Viet Cong from using the remote mountain areas as hiding places.

In the days when most Americans felt the Vietnam War was a glorious anti-Communist crusade, the Green Berets were the most celebrated of all the American troops. A song was written about them, and John Wayne starred in a movie titled *The Green Berets*, showing their success against the evil Viet Cong.

In reality, the Green Berets were highly trained professional soldiers. They often worked in twelve-man groups called A teams. Because A teams sometimes parachuted into remote areas where they worked on their own for months, they received training in survival skills and sabotage. Each A-team member had a specialty, such as light weapons, explosives, or medicine. Each was also trained in a second specialty so the unit could remain effective after taking casualties.

The A teams went into montagnard villages and tried to win them as allies. They trained montagnards in military tactics, winning their confidence by performing such medical tasks as giving vaccinations, dispensing vitamins, and pulling teeth. Often A-team members took part in ceremonies such as animal sacrifice to strengthen their bonds with the native people. As a sign of acceptance, the montagnards gave them brass bracelets, which marked their membership in the tribe. Proud of the work they did, A-team members continued to wear these bracelets long after their return to the United States.

---

grams would show that democracy had more to offer than communism. Kennedy believed that Vietnam would be a test case of this idea.

Kennedy's advisers shared his optimistic, can-do spirit. He had gathered around him men of great intellectual ability, who were later dubbed "the best and the brightest." Foremost among them was the new secretary of defense, Robert McNamara.

McNamara's brilliance was legendary. In World War II he had helped to direct the bombing of Nazi Europe. In those days before computers, it was said that McNamara carried the coordinates (exact locations) of all enemy bombing targets in his head. McNamara was confident that he could solve any problem if he was given enough information about it. He believed that statistics could tell the whole story. He wanted to know such things about Vietnam as the number of troops on both sides, the number of villages held by the government, how many people were killed or wounded, how much ammunition was required—statistics. But as *New York Times* columnist James Reston later wrote of McNamara: "Something is missing: some element of personal doubt, some respect for human weakness, some knowledge of history."

Kennedy's new secretary of state, Dean Rusk, was a hard-line anti-Communist. He had served with the U.S. Army in the Far East during World War II. After the war, he joined the State Department. There, his opposition to communism won him promotion during the years when McCarthy's witch-hunts were driving others from government service. Rusk had argued strongly in favor of American aid to the French in Vietnam. Now he was ready to commit American power to the worldwide fight against communism.

Despite their brilliance, the men around Kennedy did not understand what was really going on in Vietnam. Like Dulles, they saw it as a fight between communism and democracy. Lansdale, who had left Vietnam in 1956 after Diem's power seemed secure, had continued to follow what was happening there. Concerned, he wanted to go back, and spoke to a group of Kennedy advisers about the real nature of the conflict in Vietnam. As he spoke, he showed a razor-sharp punji stick to help them understand what guerrilla warfare was like. The advisers were not impressed, and Lansdale didn't get the post he hoped for. The "best and the brightest" thought that people who used sticks as weapons would be no match for the firepower Americans could bring to Vietnam.

There were about 900 American military advisers in Vietnam when Kennedy took office. Diem's Army of the Republic of Vietnam (ARVN) numbered more than 200,000 men, opposing a Viet Cong guerrilla force of only 17,000. Yet the ARVN seemed unable to stamp out the Viet Cong. Kennedy wanted to know why. In October 1961 he sent General Maxwell Taylor and Walt Rostow to Vietnam to look over the situation. (The "fact-finding mission" of high government officials became a ritual during the Vietnam years. McNamara alone would take ten of these trips.)

Taylor was a career military officer who had helped develop the idea of counterinsurgency. Rostow was a college professor who had taken a job under Rusk in the State Department. Rostow discussed countries like

Vietnam as if they really were dominoes—merely pieces in the worldwide game that was being played between the United States and the Soviet Union.

When Taylor and Rostow returned, they presented a simple plan—more Americans were needed in Vietnam. They wanted Kennedy to send more advisers to show the Vietnamese government and army how to improve. They also called for 10,000 American combat troops to fight the war directly.

Kennedy rejected the idea of combat troops—that was too drastic a step. But he increased the Green Beret forces—specialists in counterinsurgency—and sent more military equipment, including helicopters with American pilots, to assist the ARVN troops. By the end of 1963, there were 16,000 American military advisers in Vietnam. To handle this increase, the U.S. military headquarters in Saigon was reorganized and renamed the Military Assistance Command—Vietnam (MACV, known to the troops as "Mack-vee").

In explaining why he refused to send combat troops to Vietnam, Kennedy warned: "The troops will march in; the bands will play; the crowds will cheer; and in four days everyone will have forgotten. Then we will be told we have to send in more troops. It's like taking a drink. The effect wears off, and you have to take another."

The new U.S. advisers took a more active role in the fighting. Some went into combat with the ARVN forces. On December 22, 1961, one of them, James T. Davis, was riding in a truck with ten South Vietnamese

A South Vietnamese soldier, waiting to be flown into battle, carries a duck so that he will have something to eat. Supplies sent by the Americans to feed the troops were often diverted and sold illegally at very high prices. (Rene Burri/Magnum)

soldiers. The truck ran over a Viet Cong mine buried in the road. Davis, unhurt by the explosion, jumped out with his rifle ready. The VC were waiting in the brush alongside the road. With submachine guns, they cut down Davis and the ARVN soldiers he had been training. Davis was the first American to die in combat in Vietnam.

The Americans found that the ARVN troops were eager to learn but did not perform well in combat. They were poorly paid and poorly led. The cost of their meals was deducted from their pay. Their officers were appointed because of their family connections or their loyalty to Diem. Diem rewarded officers whose troops had low casualties—hence, they avoided risking their men in combat situations. Diem kept the best troops close to him in Saigon to prevent any attempts to overthrow him.

What the American advisers could not give the South Vietnamese was a fighting spirit equal to the Viet Cong's. One regroupee who returned south to fight with the Viet Cong wrote in his diary: "Now my life is full of hardship—not enough rice to eat nor enough salt to give a taste to my tongue, not enough clothing to keep myself warm! But in my heart I keep loyal to the Party and to the people. I am proud and happy."

Still, the U.S. advisers did help the ARVN troops win some victories against the Viet Cong. So-called "eagle flights" of combat helicopters carried crews of Americans and Vietnamese. Since few Vietnamese could fly helicopters, they went along mostly to maintain the idea that Americans were only "advising." Between themselves, American pilots called their Vietnamese co-pilots "sandbags."

At first, the armed helicopters frightened the Viet Cong, who called them dragons. The Americans grew confident. Kennedy himself, echoing the words of General Navarre at Dien Bien Phu, said in 1962, "We don't see the end of the tunnel, but I must say I don't think it is darker than it was a year ago, and in some ways [it is] lighter."

An American general told a journalist, "The Viet Cong are Vietnamese too and they've got the same failings as the government guys we're supporting. You've got to remember that these people . . . don't have the military tradition we've got." The general didn't know much about Vietnamese history. Before long, the Viet Cong were shooting down the American helicopters.

The new American advisers soon saw the difference between Diem's ARVN troops and the Viet Cong. In early 1963, ARVN units were sent to Ap Bac (pronounced Op Back), a village only forty miles southwest of

South Vietnamese soldiers leap from an American helicopter in search of hidden Viet Cong forces, 1963. (Rene Burri/Magnum)

Saigon. Their mission was to wipe out a much smaller Viet Cong force near the village. Though armed American helicopters went along to provide air support, the attack was an embarrassing and deadly failure.

ARVN commanders at Ap Bac moved their troops cautiously, ignoring the pleas of American advisers to take advantage of their superiority in weapons and numbers. When the Viet Cong shot down five of the helicopters, an ARVN commander refused to send his troops to rescue their crews, and they were machine-gunned. Three Americans were among them. Another American officer died while trying to get one of the ARVN units to move forward. The Viet Cong fought off the government troops, which gladly allowed them to escape.

The chief American adviser on the scene at Ap Bac called the action "a miserable . . . performance." Yet higher American officers in Saigon termed it a victory because the Viet Cong had left the area. Those who knew the real story realized that defeating the Viet Cong would be much tougher than Kennedy and his advisers imagined.

Part of the purpose of counterinsurgency was to win the support of the villagers of South Vietnam. They had to be persuaded that the government could protect and assist them. If the villagers were loyal to the government, the Viet Cong would have no base to work from.

One effort to protect the villagers was the "strategic hamlet" program, begun in 1962. The area around a strategic hamlet—which was part of a larger village—was to be cleared of Viet Cong. Each hamlet would be fortified with barbed wire, and the villagers armed as a "self-defense force." American aid would then provide health and sanitary facilities, education, and other benefits. These strategic hamlets would be like an oil spot in water—they would spread out to eventually include all of Vietnam.

Unfortunately, Diem's brother Ngo Dinh Nhu took charge of the program. He saw the strategic hamlets as a quick way to victory and set about building them all over the country. But he ignored the need to secure the local areas first. Writer Michael Maclear had just helicopftered into one when nearby guerrillas opened fire. Maclear described what happened next: "The hamlet defenders, youths hardly taller than their rifles, immediately threw open the fortified gate and threw down their guns." Maclear was rescued only because the American helicopter pilot saw what happened and came back to get him.

A Green Beret tries to persuade a village elder to move his people closer to an American camp, where they can be protected. (Courtesy of U.S. Army)

Another problem with the strategic hamlets was that people were sometimes forced to leave their old homes to live in a new hamlet. This practice violated the Vietnamese people's traditional loyalty to their home villages. The peasants did not want to be uprooted and separated from the places where their ancestors were buried. The new hamlet chiefs were of course appointed by the government, and they commanded no loyalty from the villagers.

Diem's government reported that it had built 4,000 strategic hamlets in 1962, with 39 percent of the population living in them. Statistics like these pleased Washington, but still the Viet Cong grew stronger.

Corruption spread through all levels of the government of South Vietnam. People appointed by Diem enriched themselves with American aid that should have been spent fighting the Viet Cong and helping the villagers. Catholics were favored over Buddhists for important government posts. Bribery became a way of life.

When American advisers tried to persuade Diem to reform his government, he would launch into one of his legendary "monologues" in which he would talk nonstop, brushing aside interruptions, for hours on end. Diem fancied himself an expert on many topics and would lecture visitors endlessly on such things as weather forecasting. When the real problems of Vietnam were raised, Diem dismissed them as rumors spread by his enemies.

As Diem's fear of enemies increased, his relatives became powerful figures. His most trusted adviser was his brother Nhu, himself an erratic character. Nhu's secret police had agents throughout the army and government sending him reports. He formed a youth organization called the Blue Shirts. When Nhu appeared at their rallies, the Blue Shirts would drop to one knee and hail him with upraised fists and shouts of loyalty.

Nhu's wife, Madame Nhu, was an attractive but vicious woman who became the "first lady" of South Vietnam. She formed her own small army of women trained in karate and enjoyed watching them demonstrate their skills against men. Madame Nhu became notorious for her campaigns against what she considered immoral behavior. She banned dancing, sentimental songs, beauty contests, and boxing matches. She closed Saigon's nightclubs and outlawed divorce. At her order, a statue of the Trung sisters—who had led one of the earliest rebellions against the

Chinese—was raised in a Saigon square. The face of one of them was unmistakably that of Madame Nhu herself.

I n 1963, opposition to Diem exploded with the "Buddhist crisis." It began over a seemingly small dispute. At a celebration honoring another of Diem's brothers, the Catholic Archbishop of Hue, white and gold Catholic flags were carried through the streets. But when Buddhists applied for permission to carry their own flags in a procession on Buddha's birthday later that year, Diem refused. An American official compared this to banning the singing of Christmas carols in the United States.

The Buddhists' long-smoldering resentment of Diem's favoritism toward Catholics now boiled over. On May 9, Buddha's birthday, Buddhists defied Diem's ban and paraded through the streets of Hue with their flags. Government troops fired on the parade and nine people died.

In the month that followed, protests against the massacre spread

June 11, 1963. Buddhist monk Quang Duc commits public suicide at a busy Saigon intersection to protest Diem's harsh treatment of the Buddhists. (AP/Wide World)

throughout the country. Diem's police raided Buddhist pagodas, looking for the organizers.

On June 11, the Buddhists staged a dramatic response to Diem's crackdown. An elderly Buddhist monk named Quang Duc (pronounced Kwong Duck) seated himself at the intersection of two of Saigon's major streets, tolling prayers on a string of beads. Younger monks doused his robes with gasoline. When they stepped back, the old monk lit a match. Immediately, he burst into flames. Without a cry of pain, he burned for ten minutes until his charred body fell apart.

The Buddhists had alerted an American photographer to the planned suicide. The photographs he took were on the front pages of the world's newspapers the following day. Many Americans became aware of Vietnam for the first time when they saw the suicide of the old monk.

Governments around the world protested Diem's treatment of the Buddhists. Diem claimed that the monk's suicide was part of a Viet Cong plot. But more Buddhists, both monks and nuns, soon followed in public suicides. Madame Nhu made more headlines when she sneered at the suicides, saying she would light the match for the "barbecues."

The suicides were a signal to all Vietnamese who opposed Diem's regime. Students took to the streets to join the protests. In Saigon, many college students were arrested, and the university was closed. Then the protest spread to high schools, where more students were arrested. By the end of the summer, the government was jailing grade-school children.

The U.S. government warned Diem that it feared he was leading the country into chaos, but Diem paid no attention.

During the summer of 1963, a new American ambassador arrived in Saigon—Henry Cabot Lodge. By now, many of Kennedy's advisers thought Diem was the problem in South Vietnam. Our ally needed a new leader. When Lodge learned that South Vietnamese army officers were planning a coup to overthrow Diem, he recommended that Washington support it.

CIA agent Lucien Conein made contact with the plotters. Using a dentist's office as a meeting place, Conein cautiously gave them advice. If they were unsuccessful, the United States did not want to be tied to them. The two leaders of the plot, Generals Duong Van Minh (pronounced Yoon Vahn Ming) and Tran Van Don (pronounced Trahn Vahn Doan), wanted firmer promises of support from the United States before they would act.

For the next two months Lodge sent cables to Washington, urging support for the planned coup. Kennedy and his advisers were not sure what to do. McNamara and General Taylor flew to Saigon on another fact-finding mission. When they returned, they gave opposite opinions on what was happening in Vietnam. Kennedy said, "You two did visit the same country, didn't you?"

In October, Lodge told the generals that the United States would not try to stop a coup. The generals took this as a green light. Time was short. They feared that Diem would learn of their plans.

On November 1, Conein's "dentist" told him the coup was beginning.

Conein went to the plotters' headquarters with a satchel full of money in case it was needed. Troops were already surrounding the presidential palace, where Diem and his brother were hiding in an underground bomb shelter. From the palace, Diem telephoned Lodge to ask what the U.S. attitude toward the "rebellion" was. Lodge said he was not well enough informed to answer.

"I have tried to do my duty," Diem said.

"I admire your courage," Lodge replied, "and your great contribution to your country." He added that he was concerned about Diem's safety. There was a pause. Diem seemed to know what this meant—the United States wanted him to surrender without a fight. Instead, Diem hung up. He and his brother escaped from the palace through a secret corridor.

The next day Diem spoke with General Minh by telephone. Minh guaranteed that Diem and his brother would be safe if they surrendered, and Diem revealed their hiding place. Minh sent an officer to pick them up in an armored car. As the officer left, Minh raised two fingers—the signal to kill them both.

Kennedy was at a meeting in Washington when the news came that Diem and Nhu had been murdered in the back of the armored car. According to Maxwell Taylor, Kennedy "rushed from the room with a look of shock and dismay on his face." Lodge had led him to think that Diem would not be killed in the coup.

Another of Diem's brothers, who was governor of the area around Hue, fled to the U.S. government office in Hue. Lodge sent an American plane, promising to take him to safety. But the plane landed in Saigon instead, and Diem's brother was turned over to the generals and later killed. Madame Nhu was more fortunate—she was in Rome at the time. Lodge allowed her children to leave Vietnam and join her there.

Three weeks later Kennedy himself was dead—shot while riding in an open car in the streets of Dallas. Americans were shocked by the death of their young leader, who had inspired them with promises of a great future. Four days of mourning, ending with Kennedy's funeral procession through Washington, D.C., left the country dazed and saddened.

For a time, Vietnam was forgotten. When Kennedy's vice-president, Lyndon Johnson, now the President, met with his staff to decide what he should do first, Vietnam was not a major concern. One of Johnson's advisers recalled, "We hardly discussed [Vietnam] because it wasn't worth discussing." But by cooperating in the assassination of Diem, the United States moved a step deeper into Vietnam.

The United States Enters the War

*I am not going to be the President who saw Southeast
Asia go the way of China.*

—Lyndon Johnson, 1963

L YNDON B. Johnson was now President of the United States. Johnson,
a Texan, was a big man with a strong personality. Earlier, as a
leading member of the Senate, he had been a skilled "arm twister,"
confident that he could settle any dispute by sitting down with
those involved and arguing it out.

Johnson was not particularly interested in foreign policy. He wanted
to solve the problems Americans had at home. When he was a young
man, he had been a schoolteacher in a small Texas town. Most of his
students were poor Mexican-Americans. He remembered them coming to
school, "most of them without any breakfast, most of them hungry. . . .
I swore then and there that if I ever had a chance to help [them] I was
going to do it."

His chance came when he became President. Johnson set the goal of
a "Great Society," in which all Americans would share in the nation's
prosperity. He announced plans for a "War on Poverty." But it was a
different war—the war in Vietnam—that would dominate his presidency
and, finally, destroy it.

As Kennedy's vice-president, Johnson had visited Vietnam in 1961.
His trip was a way of showing the Kennedy administration's support for
Diem. Johnson had showered Diem with praise, comparing him to the
great British prime minister Winston Churchill, who had led his country
to victory in World War II. When a skeptical reporter asked Johnson if he

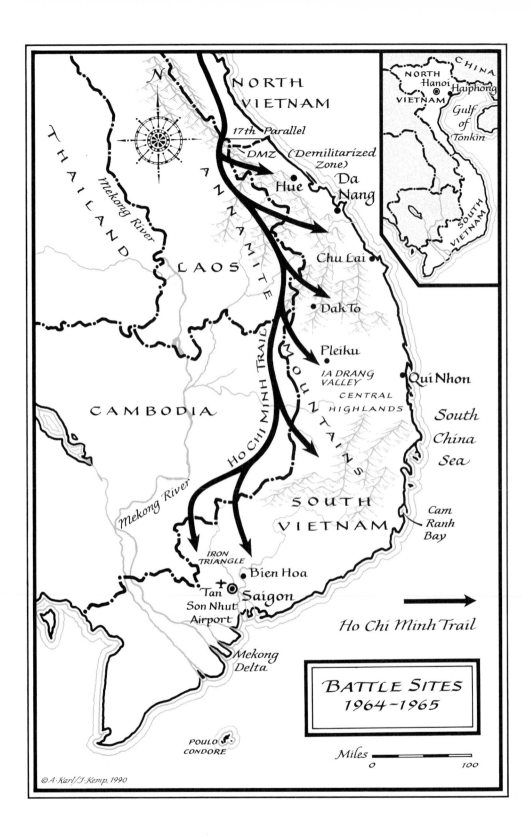

N

NORTH
VIETNAM

17th Parallel

DMZ (Demilitarized
Zone)

Hue

Da
Nang

THAILAND

Mekong River

LAOS

Chu Lai

A
N
N
A
M
I
T
E

Dak To

Pleiku

M
O
U
N
T
A
I
N
S

IA DRANG
VALLEY

CENTRAL
HIGHLANDS

Qui Nhon

CAMBODIA

Ho Chi Minh Trail

South
China
Sea

Mekong River

SOUTH
VIETNAM

Cam
Ranh
Bay

IRON
TRIANGLE

Bien Hoa

Tan
Son Nhut
Airport

Saigon

Ho Chi Minh Trail

Mekong
Delta

BATTLE SITES
1964–1965

POULO
CONDORE

Miles
0   100

CHINA

NORTH
VIETNAM

Hanoi

Haiphong

Gulf
of
Tonkin

SOUTH
VIETNAM

really meant it, Johnson replied, "Diem's the only boy we got out there." As the Americans were now to learn, there was no strong South Vietnamese leader to take his place.

The generals who had overthrown Diem began to fight among themselves for power. Throughout 1964, one military government after another rose and fell in South Vietnam. The Viet Cong took advantage of the confusion to increase their hold on the countryside.

When Johnson took office, he kept most of Kennedy's advisers, including McNamara and Rusk. They warned him that Vietnam was in danger of falling to the Communists. Johnson was determined not to let that happen. He remembered how President Truman had been blamed for the "loss" of China in 1948. Johnson did not want the loss of Vietnam on his record. He told an aide, "I am not going to be the President who saw Southeast Asia go the way of China."

Johnson was impatient. If the South Vietnamese could not win by themselves, the Americans should give them more help. His advisers had a plan all ready for him—to bomb North Vietnam. But that was a drastic step. The United States was not officially at war with North Vietnam, and Johnson needed a clear reason to bomb the North. The Gulf of Tonkin incident would provide that reason.

The Gulf of Tonkin is a part of the South China Sea just east of North Vietnam. In the summer of 1964, with secret help from U.S. forces, South Vietnamese PT boats (small, lightly armed patrol boats) began raiding North Vietnam's bases along the gulf coast. During the raids, American warships would patrol the gulf, listening to North Vietnam's military radio messages. The Americans wanted to know how quickly the North responded to the PT boat attacks.

On the night of July 30–31, 1964, South Vietnamese PT boats attacked some islands in the gulf. The American destroyer *Maddox* steamed into the area shortly after midnight on August 2. That afternoon, it sighted three North Vietnamese PT boats approaching at high speed. The boats began to fire torpedoes and machine guns at the *Maddox*. The *Maddox* fired back. Four jets from an American aircraft carrier joined the fight. One North Vietnamese boat was sunk, and the other two fled. The only damage to the *Maddox* was one bullet hole from the machine guns.

When the news reached Washington, Johnson warned North Vietnam that the United States would retaliate if there were any more attacks on its ships. Two nights later, on August 4, the *Maddox* returned to the gulf, joined by the destroyer *C. Turner Joy*. Fog made it difficult to see. The ships scanned the area with radar, but low clouds created false radar images. What actually happened that night remains shrouded in mystery— but it would be enough to cause the United States to go to war.

As the two American ships approached the area of the earlier attack, the *Maddox*'s radar operator reported unidentified objects thirty-six miles ahead. As the objects approached, the *Turner Joy*'s radar confirmed the sighting. When the radar blips were 4,000 yards away, the *Turner Joy* opened fire in their direction. No one actually saw any Vietnamese boats. Four crewmen on the *Turner Joy* said they saw the wake of a torpedo pass by. Eight American jets flew over, but could not detect any enemy vessels. The two American ships finally turned south. Neither had been hit, nor had the American planes.

Captain John Herrick, aboard the *Maddox,* said it was "doubtful" that there had been any actual attack. But higher-ranking officers farther from the scene disagreed after hearing North Vietnamese radio messages. Five thousand miles from the gulf, in Honolulu, Admiral U. S. Grant Sharp, commander of the Pacific Fleet, cabled Johnson that the North Vietnamese had defied the President's warning.

Johnson decided to strike back. He went on television to tell the American people of the North Vietnamese attack. The U.S. reply, he said, "is being given as I speak to you tonight." American jets had already taken off from aircraft carriers to bomb North Vietnam.

Only military targets were bombed—PT boat bases and an oil storage depot—and Johnson declared that the raid was a success. But General Giap had prepared for an attack, and the North's antiaircraft fire brought down two American planes. Flying one of them was Lieutenant Everett Alvarez. He was the first American pilot captured by the North Vietnamese, and he would remain a prisoner for nine years.

Now Johnson had an excuse for increasing the American involvement in Vietnam. He asked Congress to approve a resolution giving him the authority to "take all necessary measures to repel any armed attack against the forces of the United States and to prevent further aggression." On August 7, the House of Representatives passed the Gulf of Tonkin Resolution by a vote of 416 to 0. The Senate approved it the same day by a vote of 88 to 2. The only two senators to vote against the resolution were Wayne Morse of Oregon and Ernest Gruening of Alaska.

Johnson never asked Congress for a formal declaration of war. He didn't need one. In the next three years, he would send more than half a million American troops into Vietnam and stage the largest bombing campaign in the history of warfare. With the Gulf of Tonkin Resolution—and the sheer strength of his personality—Johnson was able to carry on a major war with no further authorization from Congress.

But because there was never a formal declaration of war, doubts always remained as to what our real purpose was in Vietnam. "Why are we in Vietnam?" asked those who later opposed the war. There was no clear answer, for Congress never really debated the reasons for our involvement.

The Constitution makes the President the commander of the armed forces, but it gives Congress the power to declare war—so that such a major step will not be taken without good reason. When Congress passed the Gulf of Tonkin Resolution, no one who voted for it could have guessed that it would draw the United States into one of the bloodiest wars in its history. Yet that is what happened.

Johnson waited before he used the powers that Congress had given him to widen the war. In the fall of 1964, he faced a presidential election. Johnson wanted a full term as President. His opponent was conservative Republican Senator Barry Goldwater.

All American politicians of both parties were anti-Communist, but Goldwater went further than most. He wanted to roll back Communist gains all over the world, a policy that some Americans thought was extreme. When Goldwater accepted the Republican nomination, he said, "Extremism in the defense of liberty is not a vice." In the campaign that followed, Johnson frightened Americans into thinking that Goldwater might lead the nation into nuclear war.

Johnson did not reveal his plans for Vietnam. He told one audience, "I have not thought that we were ready for American boys to do the fighting for Asian boys . . . we are not going north and drop bombs at this stage of the game, and we are not going south and run out and leave it for the Communists to take over." These words would later come back to haunt him, but in 1964 most Americans believed that Johnson was the "peace candidate." In November he won a landslide victory.

Unknown to the American public, Johnson was already taking steps to do just what he had promised not to. On the very day of the election, Johnson's advisers were drawing up plans for a major air attack on North Vietnam. Daniel Ellsberg, one of the planners, later said, "We didn't wait until the day after the election: that would have wasted time. We didn't meet the day before the election . . . because that might have leaked." Johnson kept his real plans for Vietnam secret, because he knew most Americans did not favor widening the war.

The bombing after the Gulf of Tonkin incident had not discouraged the North Vietnamese. In fact, it seemed to have the opposite effect. Johnson learned from secret reports that the first units of the North Vietnamese Army (NVA) had entered South Vietnam in August 1964. (Up until then all the fighting had been carried on by the Viet Cong.)

And the enemy grew bolder. Two days before the U.S. presidential elections, Viet Cong mortar shells hit the American airbase at Bien Hoa, close to Saigon.

South Vietnam's military government was unpopular, and street demonstrations led by Buddhists and students continued. The government of South Vietnam seemed ready to collapse. In Washington, many believed that the only way to prevent that was to bring in American troops. Johnson agonized over the decision. Like Kennedy, he was getting conflicting advice over what kind of pressure to apply, where, and how much.

The trigger to action came on February 7, 1965. On that day, the Viet Cong attacked Camp Holloway, an American Green Beret camp near Pleiku (pronounced Play-koo). Pleiku was in the Central Highlands, the area of South Vietnam between the coast and the Annamite Mountains.

February 7 was the end of Tet, the Vietnamese New Year, and there had been a truce in the fighting. Things seemed peaceful until 2 A.M., when out of the darkness mortar shells suddenly rained down on the American camp. At nearly the same time, Viet Cong "sappers"—commandos armed with satchel bombs—charged onto the camp's airstrip and blew up several parked aircraft. Another group attacked the officers' villa, thrusting pole charges—explosives on the ends of bamboo poles—against the walls.

The surprise attack killed 8 Americans and wounded 109. Ten aircraft were destroyed. A detailed map of the camp was found on the body of one of the attackers. And the Americans learned that the enemy mortar guns had been hidden in a nearby village for days. Clearly, the attack was the result of careful planning and preparation. Yet the Americans had received no hint of it—showing that many local Vietnamese were in sympathy with the Viet Cong.

Johnson's national security adviser, McGeorge Bundy, was on a fact-finding trip to Vietnam at the time. He flew to Pleiku to see the damage. Bundy, the former dean of Harvard College, had urged both Kennedy and Johnson to move cautiously in Vietnam. But the bloody scene at Pleiku sickened and angered him. He called the President and asked for immediate retaliation. Less than fourteen hours later, navy jets left aircraft carriers on a bombing mission against North Vietnam. On the way back to Washington, Bundy wrote a report urging further action against the North. When he presented the report, Johnson said, "Well, they made a believer out of you, didn't they? A little fire will do that."

Despite the U.S. bombing, the VC attacked again three days later. At Qui Nhon (pronounced Kwee Nyon), 280 miles up the coast from Saigon, guerrillas shot their way into a hotel used as a barracks for U.S. soldiers and killed 23 Americans.

Johnson decided that the time had come to show he meant business. Instead of responding only when attacks took place, he ordered constant bombing of the North. The bombing operation, known as Rolling Thunder, began in early March 1965, and would continue until 1968.

In the years of Rolling Thunder, Johnson followed a "carrot and stick" policy. The "stick" was continued bombing of the North. The "carrot" was a promise of economic aid. Johnson offered a billion-dollar development plan that North Vietnam could share in, if the fighting stopped.

"Old Ho can't turn me down," Johnson once said. He saw the Vietnamese as people like Americans—they would respond to his offers of aid because they wanted a better life for themselves. Since taking control of the North in 1954, Ho had built new factories to help improve his country's economy. Johnson felt that by threatening to bomb these factories, he could force Ho to give in. But Ho valued his dream of a united Vietnam more than the factories or the promise of American aid. In 1965, Pham Van Dong, now prime minister of North Vietnam, said the only basis for peace would be the sharing of power between the Viet Cong and the South Vietnamese government. Johnson could not agree to this, and the bombing went on.

A North Vietnamese antiair-craft unit ready to defend the North against President Johnson's Rolling Thunder bombing campaign, which lasted from 1965 till 1968. (The Bettmann Archive)

General William Westmoreland had become the new American commander of MACV in June 1964. "Westy" was tall and trim, square-jawed and self-assured. He seemed to be the ideal military commander. He had been First Captain of his class at West Point, and his career had moved steadily upward ever since.

Westmoreland believed that Rolling Thunder would bring more Viet Cong attacks on military bases in the South. American troops would be needed to defend them. Johnson agreed. On March 8, 1965, 3,500 marines—the first American combat troops in Vietnam—arrived near Da Nang, a port city 100 miles south of the DMZ. The mayor of the city met them with a group of young Vietnamese women who draped garlands of orchids around their necks. To these South Vietnamese, and to most Americans, the marines had come to save their country from communism.

Others had misgivings. Maxwell Taylor, a former general himself, was now the American ambassador to South Vietnam. He had developed the idea of counterinsurgency that Kennedy thought would work in Vietnam. Taylor called the American combat troops "the nose of the camel"—meaning that once the nose of the camel got into the tent, it was impossible to keep the whole camel out. The idea of counterinsurgency had been to train the people of Vietnam to defend themselves—not to have large numbers of Americans do the fighting.

Taylor's warning was not heeded. Once the American troops began to arrive, they gradually took over the fighting. Counterinsurgency was forgotten, and the war now became an American one—planned by American generals and carried out mainly by American troops.

Westmoreland developed a threefold strategy for victory. First, American forces would go into enemy-held areas and use superior weapons and firepower to clean them out. Once the area was clear, South Vietnamese troops would be sent in to hold it. In the third stage, American

Marines from H Company, 2nd Battalion, keep their rifles and their cigarettes dry as they cross a river. The first American combat soldiers arrived in Vietnam in March 1965. (Courtesy of U.S. Marine Corps)

economic and technical help would win the loyalty of the rural villages in the South.

As Taylor had warned, the plan required many more American troops. At Westmoreland's request, more American soldiers poured into Vietnam. Six weeks after the marines landed at Da Nang, there were 82,000 American marine and army troops in the country. By the end of 1965, there were 184,000. As quickly as that, without any real public debate, the United States became deeply involved in Vietnam.

From this point on there was no turning back. Once the United States decided to defend South Vietnam with its own forces, its prestige was on the line. To send all these troops meant that the United States must win a clear victory. To withdraw without one would be a humiliating defeat—too humiliating for any president to consider. The United States was now deep in the tunnel of Vietnam, and there was no way for it to turn around.

One encouraging sign was that a stable government finally took control of South Vietnam in 1965, led by forty-two-year-old General Nguyen

Two young residents of a South Vietnamese village enjoy a ride on the shoulders of an American marine. (The Bettmann Archive)

Van Thieu (pronounced Noo-yen Vahn Tyoo). It would last until South Vietnam fell in 1975. Thieu's rise to power had been a quiet one. During his career, he had hopped from one side to another, allying himself with whatever group seemed to be most powerful. He fought with the Viet Minh in 1945, but quit after a year to join the French. Trained in the French military academy in Vietnam, he became a convert to Catholicism. After the French left, Thieu was one of the officers who formed the nucleus of Diem's army. Diem sent him to the United States for further training at the army base at Fort Leavenworth, Kansas. But when Diem began to lose control of the country, Thieu joined the plotters who overthrew him.

In the flip-flop of governments that followed, Thieu remained in the background. He kept from making important enemies, and thus became the compromise choice to lead the country. South Vietnam's other generals felt comfortable with him—and under his leadership, corruption became a way of life. Thieu kept power by arranging for nearly every official down to the village level to get a share of the massive American aid that was pouring into the country.

Nguyen Cao Ky (pronounced Noo-yen Cow Key) was Thieu's prime minister and later his vice-president. Ky was the most colorful of South Vietnam's military leaders. He often appeared in a purple flight suit with a lavender scarf, sporting two pearl-handled revolvers on his belt. A skilled and daring pilot, he liked to call himself the Warlord of the Air.

Born in 1930 near Hanoi, Ky had served with the French as a fighter pilot against the Viet Minh. During Diem's regime, Ky flew secret bombing missions for the CIA and, like Thieu, received training in the United States. But his unpredictable behavior made his fellow generals wary of him— keeping him out of the top job.

By August 1965, the marines at Da Nang had spread out north and south along the coast. They had faced brief hit-and-run attacks, but had not located any large body of enemy forces. On August 15, a Viet Cong deserter revealed that the VC were massing for a major attack on the marine camp at Chu Lai (pronounced Chew Lie), south of Da Nang. The marines decided to strike first.

General Lewis Walt, marine commander in Vietnam, designed a classic land-and-sea marine assault—Operation Starlite. Marine forces on land would encircle the Viet Cong force, cutting off their escape routes and pushing them toward the sea. Other marines waiting offshore would land and shut the trap. Navy ships in the South China Sea would add their firepower to the attack. Finally, air support—helicopter gunships and planes—would lay down bombs and machine-gun fire on enemy positions.

On August 17 and 18, the marines closed their trap on the VC forces. But the VC lived up to their billing as fierce and clever fighters. One of the marine helicopter landing sites was next to a hill that was occupied by a VC battalion. The VC let the first helicopters land without revealing

June 1965. Marines near Da Nang hold their ears while firing mortar shells at Viet Cong forces nearby. (Courtesy of U.S. Marine Corps)

their presence. When others arrived, the VC opened fire on them with rocket-propelled grenades and machine guns.

This was a favorite tactic of the Viet Cong—it cut off the first unit on the ground and left them helpless. This time, however, the VC were no match for marine airpower. Helicopter gunships pounded the VC, and with the help of tanks, the marines finally took the hill.

The Battle of Chu Lai was a triumph for the marines. They had, as planned, crushed the VC forces. The battle showed that combined air, sea, and land firepower could defeat the Viet Cong guerrillas. The Viet Cong learned the same lesson. They waited until the monsoon season, when heavy rains made airpower less effective, before fighting the marines again.

Meanwhile U.S. army units were also pouring into Vietnam. Among them was the First Cavalry Division, whose responsibility was the area around Pleiku in the Central Highlands.

The First Cav was not alone in the area. North Vietnamese Army forces were arriving by way of the Ho Chi Minh Trail. North Vietnam hoped to score a major victory before the American troop build-up became too large. Its plan was to drive across the Central Highlands to the sea and cut South Vietnam in two. The stage was set for the first battle between U.S. troops and regular North Vietnamese forces.

On October 19, 1965, NVA soldiers attacked a small Green Beret camp thirty miles from Pleiku. The NVA knew that a relief force would come to rescue the camp. They waited in ambush along the expected route of the relief force. But the Americans foiled the plan. They simply flew over the ambush sites in helicopters, and along with artillery and a battalion of the First Cavalry, they drove off the enemy.

However, the battle was only beginning. General Westmoreland decided to go after the retreating NVA. The month-long fighting that followed became known as the Battle of the Ia Drang (pronounced Yah Drahn) Valley.

The Ia Drang Valley is an area of dense jungle—making it an ideal hiding place for the enemy. The South Vietnamese had long known that to pursue their enemy into such an area was to invite disaster. The enemy could hide until an approaching column of troops was inside their "killing zone." Explosives could be set up along a trail and set off by a hidden scout. Soldiers who weren't killed by the explosives would then be mowed down by machine gunners hidden in the underbrush.

The Americans had a new way to counter these tactics. First they would send in low-flying planes and helicopters to draw enemy fire. Once the enemy positions were known, artillery and bombs could be directed at them. After that, American troops would land to wipe out the remaining forces. Called reconnaissance by fire, this method was not a favorite of the American pilots who had to fly over as decoys.

The Americans carried out this plan in the Ia Drang Valley. So many bombs fell on the enemy positions that it seemed nothing there could possibly survive. But when the American troops landed to mop up, the enemy popped out of tunnels and "spider holes" and cut them down with machine-gun fire. The landing zone, or LZ, was a "hot" one—meaning that the first soldiers down often faced brutal enemy fire. They had to hold the LZ by returning fire until the rest of their forces could land.

Robert Mason, a helicopter pilot in the Ia Drang battle, described what it was like to take a helicopter full of "grunts" (foot soldiers) into a hot LZ:

> At 100 feet above the trees . . . the door gunners started firing. They shot into the trees at the edge of the clearing, into bushes, anywhere they suspected the enemy was hiding. There was no return fire . . . [The troops] were growling and yelling behind me, psyched for battle. . . . As our skids hit the ground, so did the boots of the growling troops. At the same instant, the uniformed regulars from the North decided to spring their trap. From at least three different directions, they opened up on . . . the off-loading grunts with machine-gun crossfire. The LZ was suddenly alive with their screaming bullets. . . . The grunts weren't even making it to the trees. They had leapt out, screaming murderously, but now they dropped all around us, dying and dead. . . . I saw the sand spurt up in front of me as bullets tore into the ground.

This was the U.S. Army's introduction to combat in Vietnam. More than two hundred soldiers died in the Battle of the Ia Drang Valley. Even so, they fought bravely, and the NVA forces were temporarily driven out of the valley.

The NVA survivors fled east to safety in Cambodia. Westmoreland was not allowed to send his men after them, because Cambodia and Laos were, officially, neutral nations. For most of the war, crossing the border into those neighboring countries was one way the enemy could avoid Westmoreland's "search-and-destroy" missions—although U.S. planes bombed the Ho Chi Minh Trail in both countries. These hiding places were among the many things that frustrated American military commanders. They were fighting a war with new rules.

ABOVE: *Enemy snipers hid in "spider holes" like this one, waited for an American patrol to pass by, then popped out and gunned them down. (Courtesy of U.S. Army)*

BELOW: *November 1965. The strain of battle shows on the weary, unshaven face of this U.S. soldier as he moves cautiously through the underbrush in the Ia Drang Valley. (AP/Wide World)*

THE CAVALRY RETURNS

Until the beginning of the twentieth century, cavalry soldiers, mounted on horses, were an effective part of warfare. They were more formidable than foot soldiers and they could move more swiftly. But modern artillery and armored tanks made the cavalry obsolete.

However, in the 1950s American military planners began to think that helicopters could serve the same purpose as the old cavalry. Vietnam would be the testing ground for this "airmobile" idea. Staggering numbers of helicopters flew Americans to every part of the country where the enemy was operating. If there were no open spaces for the helicopters to land, one could be created by dropping a "daisy cutter"—a 15,000-pound bomb that could clear an area 300 feet in diameter.

The twin-rotor CH-21 transport helicopter, nicknamed the Flying Banana for its curved shape. (National Archives)

A CH-46 Sea Knight supply helicopter.
(Courtesy of U.S. Marine Corps)

Many kinds of helicopters were used for different purposes. The troops had nicknames for all of them. Huge transport helicopters, such as the CH-47, or Chinook, flew in the heavy artillery guns and tons of supplies and ammunition used when setting up a fire base.

In major operations, large helicopters flew in fresh troops. In the war's early years, the most common of these transport copters was the twin-rotor CH-21, nicknamed the Flying Banana for its curved shape. Later, the Sikorsky HH-53, called the Jolly Green Giant, took over the job of carrying troops. With their heavier firepower, including missiles, the Jolly Green Giants could also provide firepower from the air to aid forces on the ground. They flew into enemy territory to rescue downed pilots. Refueled in the air, they could hover over an area for hours, using machine guns to keep away the enemy until the downed pilots could reach a harness lowered to pick them up.

To the ground troops, the most welcome sight in Vietnam was a Huey—the UH-1 helicopter. Armed with machine guns and rockets, the Huey came to the rescue of soldiers in trouble, sometimes flying at speeds over 200 miles an hour. The unmistakable "whop-whop" of its single overhead rotor blade was the sound that said, "The cavalry is coming."

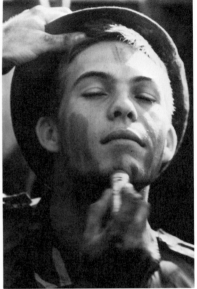

CLOCKWISE: *Three faces of battle: A soldier in the field keeps his rifle ready even at mealtimes. (Courtesy of U.S. Army) A Navy SEAL, or sea-air-land commando, is camouflaged with greasepaint for a night mission into enemy territory. (Courtesy of U.S. Navy) A paratrooper huddles under his poncho during a rainstorm. (Army News Features)*

CHAPTER SEVEN

A New Kind of War

"You know you never defeated us on the battlefield,"
said the American colonel.
The North Vietnamese colonel pondered this
remark a moment. "That may be so," he replied,
"but it is also irrelevant."

—Conversation in Hanoi, April 1975

THE United States proved at Chu Lai and in the Ia Drang Valley that it could defeat the enemy in major battles. In fact, neither the Viet Cong nor the North Vietnamese Army was ever strong enough to drive the Americans from the country by military force.

However, the enemy did not have to defeat the Americans in battle. They could win merely by staying alive in large enough numbers to remain active in South Vietnam—killing U.S. soldiers, as they had killed the French, until the Americans tired of the war.

Westmoreland's strategy was similar. He planned to use search-and-destroy missions to kill enough of the enemy to stop them from attacking the South Vietnamese government. This strategy was called attrition—the idea being to make the cost in lives so high that the goal would not be worth it.

Westmoreland continued to request, and receive, more troops to carry on this war of attrition. At the end of 1966, there were 385,300 American troops in Vietnam. A year later, the number had risen to almost half a million.

In many ways, the Vietnam War was unlike any the United States had ever fought before. Earlier wars, such as World War II, had been fought between armies who controlled the territory behind them. The places where the armies met were called fronts, and when one side drove the other's front back, it increased its hold on the enemy's territory.

Villagers pass through a checkpoint under the watchful eyes of U.S. soldiers. It was often difficult for the soldiers to tell friendly Vietnamese from the enemy because both dressed in the same black "pajamas." (National Archives)

That was not the case in Vietnam. There was no front line. American soldiers were flown in to drive the enemy away and "clear" an area. The enemy troops hid or fled while the Americans were there, and then flowed back in again when the Americans left to clear another area. American troops were not numerous enough to hold all areas of the country at the same time. Frequently, a cleared area was back in enemy hands within a few days. This was frustrating to the American troops and puzzling to the American people.

The original plan of having South Vietnamese soldiers hold areas that Americans had taken was seldom carried out. South Vietnam's military forces, despite all the attempts to train and equip them, were not very good. Around 20 percent of ARVN soldiers deserted in *each* of the years 1965 and 1966. Americans who went on missions with the South Vietnamese army called them "search-and-avoid" missions. To U.S. servicemen, the big question was, "Why don't the Vietnamese fight the VC like the VC fight the Vietnamese?"

A more serious problem was that it was often difficult for Americans to tell friend from enemy. The Viet Cong were South Vietnamese. They did not wear uniforms, but instead dressed in the same black "pajamas" that all peasants wore. They could blend in with the rest of the population. Many of the Viet Cong—both men and women—worked by day in the rice paddies and went out with their rifles at night.

Because of Westmoreland's strategy of attrition, the measure of success became the "body count"—the number of enemy soldiers killed. McNamara used it to calculate progress. At first it was supposed to be a count of the enemy bodies found on the battlefield. When American officers realized that reports of high body counts pleased their superiors, some began to include "probable kills"—an estimate of enemy dead that had been taken away for burial.

The body count became an obsession. One major-general set a quota—each unit in his command *had* to report a certain number of enemy killed. Any villagers who had been killed by bombing or artillery were counted as enemy dead, whether or not they were known to be VC. Battlefield commanders began to dig up cemeteries to add to the body count, and Westmoreland had to order that only fresh bodies could be counted. American officials constantly cited these numbers to show that the United States was winning the war, but in truth the statistics were unreliable. A later survey among officers who served in Vietnam showed that some simply made up high body counts.

Another key problem in fighting the war was the decision to limit the combat duty of U.S. Army enlisted men (non-officers) to 365 days. Marines served 13 months. In World War II, soldiers served "for the duration"—as long as the war lasted. They were part of a mission that they would see through to the end.

In Vietnam, because of the one-year policy, some American soldiers set a personal goal of "keeping their dog tags together." The dog tags were two metal identification disks that each soldier wore. If he was killed, one dog tag was taken and sent to headquarters; the other was left on the body. Keeping them together meant staying alive. Soldiers carried calendars marked with their DEROS—Date of Expected Return from Overseas. They crossed off each day that passed. As the date approached, soldiers

An American fire base in the countryside. Whenever possible, fire bases were built on high, easily defended ground. (Courtesy of U.S. Army)

became known as "short-timers"—and grew less willing to take chances.

In addition, just when the soldiers had become experienced in fighting a guerrilla war, their tour of duty ended and they went back to "the World"—the United States—on the "Freedom Bird." Fresh and inexperienced soldiers took their place. As one American officer put it: "We didn't fight ten years in Vietnam. We fought one year ten times."

Thousands of noncombat troops went to Vietnam to support the fighting men in the field. Truck drivers, mechanics, engineers, carpenters, computer operators, and headquarters personnel were all part of the American war effort, as were the many sailors on board ships in the South China Sea. War matériel—weapons, tanks, trucks, and ammunition—as well as tons of food, medicine, uniforms, and tents were brought across the Pacific by plane and ship. These supplies then had to be distributed to the troops throughout Vietnam. All this required thousands of supply clerks to handle the millions of pieces of paper that told where everything was and where it was going.

Vietnam was a land of farms and rice paddies. It had no facilities for the huge numbers of Americans who poured into the country. So American workers made their own. They built bases throughout South Vietnam and enlarged existing airfields. For a time, one of these airfields, Tan Son Nhut airbase outside Saigon, had more air traffic than any other airport in the world.

The largest base built by Americans was at Cam Ranh (pronounced Kam Ran) Bay, where an entire new port was erected to handle supplies coming in from the States. Cam Ranh Bay, about 200 miles northeast of Saigon, was only a small fishing village with a single pier in 1963. It soon became one of the world's greatest deep-water ports. It included two air-strips—one concrete, one aluminum matting—that could handle the largest cargo planes ever built. There were more than two and a half million square feet of warehouse space for ammunition alone—equal to about twenty-five K mart stores.

Cam Ranh Bay was like a small American city. It had its own dairy, hospital, cold-storage area, and electric generating plants. There was housing for more than 20,000 soldiers, pilots, and officers. Everything—cement, air conditioners, Coca-Cola—was brought in from the United States. Here, as on other American bases, life was made as comfortable as possible. Recreational areas for the troops included bars, nightclubs, outdoor movie screens, and pizza parlors.

Another function of support troops was to guard military targets—not only the bases and airfields, but also roads, railways, and bridges. The guards had to remain whether or not enemy forces were active in the area. During the Vietnam War there were about 10 U.S. support soldiers for each combat soldier. That meant that when the American strength reached its peak of 500,000 men, there were only about 50,000 soldiers actively fighting. Thus, even though American troops far outnumbered the enemy, the number of fighting forces was about the same on either side—because almost every Viet Cong and NVA soldier fought in combat.

Though the United States was a larger country than Vietnam, it was not prepared to fight a total war. Johnson refused to call up the reserves—those men who had previously completed military service and were on stand-by in case of war. He felt that to use these forces would create a storm of American protest against the war. By contrast, North Vietnam could call on all its people—male and female—to help in the war effort.

The North Vietnamese matched the American troop build-up with one of their own. "You will kill ten of our men," Ho Chi Minh had told a French general at the beginning of the first Indochina war, "but we will kill one of yours, and in the end it is you that will tire." Now, Premier Pham Van Dong told an American journalist, "We are preparing for a long war. How many years would you say? Ten, twenty. . . . What do you think about twenty? The younger generation will fight better than we."

General Giap had beaten the French with an army that began with 34 volunteers. Since then, he had built a modern, professional fighting force. By 1964, he had 250,000 men prepared for combat; the number would nearly double by 1968. Many remained in the North because of the fear that the United States would invade. But those who went south matched the numbers of Americans who were actually fighting in the field.

North Vietnam needed fewer supply troops than the Americans did—mostly porters who toted ammunition down the Ho Chi Minh Trail, sometimes using bicycles. The North Vietnamese soldier carried his own

American soldiers land on the coast of the South China Sea in an operation against enemy forces hiding in the nearby hills. (The Bettmann Archive)

weapons and rice supplies, and once in South Vietnam, he would get his food from the villagers. He didn't expect pizza parlors or air-conditioned barracks.

What he did expect was to fight, not just for a year, but until victory was won. Each unit of North Vietnamese troops had a "political officer" whose purpose was to keep their fighting spirit high. The officers continually reminded the soldiers that they were fighting to bring freedom and unity to their country. They stressed Vietnam's long history of resisting foreign rule. The rallying cry for the North Vietnamese was *dau tranh* (pronounced Dow Trang)—"struggle." *Dau tranh* meant struggling both against the enemy and against oneself. A soldier must constantly be on guard against discouraging thoughts, laziness, and careless actions.

At first, much of the fighting between Americans and Viet Cong took place in the Central Highlands—the large, tree-covered plateau in the center of South Vietnam. Westmoreland concentrated his forces there because they were sparsely populated and he wanted to avoid civilian casualties. He sent huge search-and-destroy missions through the highlands, looking for the enemy forces that were thought to be using the area as a base.

The inland tropical jungles were so thick that men could see only a few yards ahead. Streams and rivers that crossed the area suddenly dropped down sheer cliffs in spectacular waterfalls. In valleys between high hills were thickets of bamboo and fields of head-high elephant grass—perfect places to conceal enemy troops from American spotter planes.

There were few roads in the highlands, and those that existed were likely to be booby-trapped with land mines. Helicopters flew soldiers into distant areas, where they spread out and cut their way through the jungles and grasslands step by step. But the Viet Cong were usually aware of the American patrols long before they arrived, so they hid until the Americans passed by.

Farther west were the jungle-covered Annamite Mountains, where only the native montagnards knew the paths. Here, Green Beret forces operated, living among the tribes so that they could alert distant command headquarters by radio if a North Vietnamese force was crossing the mountains into South Vietnam.

The northern border of South Vietnam was the DMZ, the forty-mile-wide demilitarized zone set up by the Geneva Accords. United States Marines patrolled the area, but they were unable to keep the North Vietnamese from slipping through the dense jungles and crossing the line. In 1967, the Americans tried to build an "electronic fence" across the DMZ. Sensor devices called "people sniffers" would tell when enemy forces were near. But the fence proved costly and unworkable. Buffaloes and other animals could set off the sensors, bringing huge American air strikes down on jungles where there were no enemy troops.

Farther south, in the Mekong Delta, the Viet Cong had for years controlled areas very close to Saigon itself. Westmoreland moved to clean them out, an assignment that required a kind of warfare different from the fighting done in the highlands. Because the Mekong River formed a network of streams, the delta region was covered with swamps. Walking through these swamps was like wading in oatmeal to the American troops. Because their feet were wet almost constantly, they developed terrible cases of jungle rot—a fungus disease that eats away the skin of the feet.

To enable its troops to move swiftly through the delta, the United States brought in a fleet of flat-bottomed river boats. These "riverine forces" swept up and down the streams, using flame throwers to destroy jungle growth that could hide an enemy waiting in ambush. They stopped to check sampans—small native boats—for enemy supplies. The Vietnamese sometimes floated bomb-carrying sampans toward the American boats. The Americans had to decide within seconds whether an oncoming sampan was a booby trap or a boatload of friendly fishermen. When there was any uncertainty, the Americans fired. As many cynical soldiers said, "If it's dead and it's Vietnamese, it's VC." Fishermen or not, they were added to the body count.

In 1967, the Americans swept into a forested area nicknamed the Iron Triangle, only twenty miles northwest of Saigon. They found extensive tunnel systems, in some places four levels deep, where the Viet Cong were safe from American bombs. Inside were hospitals, storage areas, mess halls, and sleeping quarters.

The American soldiers dropped hand grenades and smoke bombs into the holes, but the tunnels twisted and turned to provide a defense against such attacks. To clear them completely, the Americans had to climb inside and fight the war underground.

It was a hair-raising job. The men had to crawl through the twisting, narrow tunnels, moving forward inch by inch, never knowing what was around the next bend. Special squads of Americans volunteered for the task, calling themselves "tunnel rats."

ABOVE: *A member of the riverine forces fires on a boat that is apparently empty but which might in fact be booby-trapped with explosives. (The Bettmann Archive)*
RIGHT: *A "tunnel rat" crawls slowly underground in search of Viet Cong. In the dark he might find anything from a booby trap to a huge supply of weapons and food. (Courtesy of U.S. Army)*

The tunnel rats went underground with flashlights, pistols, and knives. The task could take hours and required strong nerves. At any minute, a bullet might come out of the darkness—and shots fired inside such small spaces were deafening. Some tunnel rats thought they had been hit in the head even when the shots missed.

The Viet Cong often planted booby traps in the tunnels. These could be as simple as a bundle of punji sticks or a grenade attached to a trip wire. The VC also used insects and snakes as sentries. A box of spiders or scorpions would be set overhead to flop open when someone bumped it. Poisonous vipers, small but deadly, were encased in bamboo tubes. When someone brushed against the tube, it would open. Tunnel rats called the vipers one-step, two-step, or three-step snakes—depending on how far a man could go before dying of its bite.

Huge supplies of weapons and food were found in tunnels around the village of Cu Chi (pronounced Koo Chee), only fifteen miles northwest of Saigon. After blowing up the tunnels and supplies, Americans used Rome plows—enormous bulldozers—to strip the land bare of trees, so that future VC activity could be seen from the air. The blade on a Rome plow could cut through a three-foot-thick tree.

The search-and-destroy missions, no matter where they were, took a heavy toll on American lives. In 1965, 1,369 Americans died in Vietnam. The following year, 5,008 died, and the year after that, 9,377. Though TV news programs in the United States reported much higher body counts for the enemy, it was American bodies that mattered most to the people back home. They began to realize that their sons, husbands, and brothers were dying in a war in which "Asian boys" were supposed to be doing the fighting.

President Johnson and his advisers continued to hope that Rolling Thunder would win the war. Through 1966 and 1967, more than 1,000 Vietnamese were killed every week in American bombing raids. In 1966 alone, more than 8,000 buildings were destroyed.

But American bombs only hardened the Vietnamese people's deter-

North Vietnamese youngsters clean out individual air-raid shelters in downtown Hanoi. These one-person shelters were everywhere, like underground phone booths. (The Bettmann Archive)

mination, and thousands of North Vietnamese worked to repair the damage. They built bridges that lay just under the surface of rivers, so that they could not be seen from the air but could be used by trucks. They built enough bomb shelters to hold every one of their eighteen million people, including many individual shelters five feet deep and three feet in diameter. These one-person shelters were everywhere, like underground phone booths, for people to jump into when the air-raid sirens went off.

In smaller towns, people dug huge underground caves as shelters. Whole villages lived underground for much of the day, emerging only at night to tend the rice paddies. Hospitals, schools, and dining halls were all underground. Babies were born who never saw the sun as they grew up— knowing only the dim illumination of light bulbs that lined the ceilings of the caves. The slogan in the North was "Prepare for the worst"—an American invasion. More than a million people were armed with old-fashioned rifles, and schoolgirls were trained to use bayonets.

The Soviet Union sent aid to its Communist ally. With Soviet anti-aircraft missiles, sometimes manned by Soviet soldiers, the North Vietnamese shot down more than nine hundred American planes in the Rolling Thunder campaign. The United States had paid more to build these planes than the North lost from the damage they caused.

American helicopters and planes always went to rescue downed pilots who had parachuted to safety, but Vietnamese villagers sometimes captured the pilots first. One villager, then a boy, wrote later of one capture:

> I was watching the planes attack and I saw plumes of white smoke streaming out of one of them. Then the parachute came open and he began to come down . . . he landed in the open area next to my house. I ran to see along with all the kids in the neighborhood. . . . Everybody was gathering around him shouting. Some of the people tied his hands. Somebody took his pistol and somebody else took his watch. . . . They took off his shoes, too. . . . It was common knowledge that Americans couldn't run without their shoes on . . . the kids began to throw clods of dirt and stones at the pilot . . . I knew it was [forbidden to do this], but I didn't care. I was trying to find good rocks so I could really hurt him.

American bombing was not confined to the North. President Johnson also targeted the Ho Chi Minh Trail in Laos. The Vietnamese had gradually built it into a network of roads, lined with underground shelters and hospitals. At night trucks passed along the trail, carrying troops and supplies. The dense forests hid them from American planes; where necessary, the Vietnamese tied treetops together. They built trucks out of papier-mâché as dummy targets. Here, as elsewhere, enemy antiaircraft guns took their toll of American pilots. Many of the pilots shot down over Laos were listed as missing and were never accounted for.

Despite the bombing, the Ho Chi Minh Trail continued to expand. By 1967, twenty thousand NVA soldiers were coming south along the trail each month.

American bombs also fell throughout the land we were defending—South Vietnam. Bombing strikes were called in before and during American attacks. Sometimes the targets were simply areas where enemy troops were thought to be hiding. Efforts were made to clear out friendly Vietnamese before the attacks, but even when villagers escaped, their homes and rice paddies were destroyed.

Of all the planes used in the bombing attacks, the most powerful were the B-52s. They could fly 7,500 miles without refueling, making it possible for them to take off from bases far out in the Pacific Ocean, drop their deadly cargo over Vietnam, and return to safety. They flew so high that they could neither be seen nor heard by anyone on the ground. So when

An air-raid shelter near Hanoi, North Vietnam. Children wear wicker helmets as protection against splinters and shell fragments. (The Bettmann Archive)

AGENT ORANGE

Several kinds of chemicals were used in the defoliation program that was intended to wipe out enemy hiding places in jungles and grasslands. These chemicals were stored in barrels marked with different colors to make it easy to tell them apart. The sprays were known as Agent Orange, Agent Purple, and so forth. Agent Orange proved to have tragic, unforeseen side effects.

At the time, the U.S. government said that people in the sprayed areas—both villagers and soldiers—would not be harmed by the chemicals. But by the late 1960s, babies born to Vietnamese women were showing a high rate of birth defects. Agent Orange had been used in the areas where they lived. Agent Orange was partly made up of a chemical called dioxin. When the U.S. government tested dioxin on mice, it was found to cause birth defects.

By then, more than 150,000 gallons of Agent Orange were being sprayed every month over South Vietnam. In January 1971, the Defense Department ordered the spraying stopped, but the damage had already been done.

The suffering caused by Agent Orange was not limited to Vietnamese. American soldiers on the ground were sprayed by Agent Orange. After they returned home, the children they fathered also had a high rate of birth defects. Many soldiers developed skin cancer and other diseases, sometimes years after they returned from Vietnam. These veterans received compensation from the U.S. government. But they had to sue the government to get it, something that caused them much bitterness.

their bombs hit, it seemed like the earth had suddenly exploded for no reason. Each bomb weighed as much as 750 pounds, and its destructive power was massive.

A North Vietnamese soldier who went through a B-52 attack said: "It was like a giant earthquake. The whole area was filled with fire and smoke. Trees were falling all around. My shelter collapsed on me, although it hadn't been hit—I felt as if I were sitting in a metal case which someone was pounding on with a hammer."

Bombers could not find the enemy when he hid in forests, jungles, and tall elephant grass. So the Americans tried to destroy these hiding places by flying over and spraying chemicals on the trees and plants—a plan known as defoliation. The defoliation operation began during the Kennedy administration. The motto of the American pilots who carried out the missions was: "Only we can prevent forests." Later, the program was expanded to destroy food crops in Viet Cong–held areas. Between the bombs and the defoliants, parts of South Vietnam began to look like a wasteland. Even today, some of the land remains too poisoned to allow anything to grow.

Gaining the support of the villagers was also part of the new kind of war the Americans were fighting. About eight of every ten South Vietnamese lived in the countryside. These were the people from whom the VC drew their recruits, their food, and their strength. In many areas, the Viet Cong were strong enough to collect an annual tax and part of the rice harvest.

American advisers, both military and civilian, went to the Vietnamese countryside, trying to find the key to the "hearts and minds" of the villagers. They trained South Vietnamese officials to imitate the Viet Cong by living among the villagers. Few were brave enough to do so, because they became special targets of the Viet Cong, and many were killed.

The Americans tried to get the villagers to move out of Viet Cong–held areas. With American aid, the South Vietnamese government built "New Life hamlets" which offered schools, health-care centers, and other social services. But the Vietnamese didn't want to leave the villages where their ancestors were buried and their families had lived for generations. Moreover, the New Life hamlets still had to be protected, and the South Vietnamese army was often not up to the task.

Sometimes the problems stemmed from American ignorance of Vietnamese life. Luther C. Benton III was a member of the navy hospital corps that developed health programs in the villages. Village chiefs often came to him with requests for more than medical supplies. One village leader wanted a pig. Benton searched his catalog in vain and finally wrote "pig" on the order form. Two weeks later, two pigs arrived from the United States. They were much larger than those common in Vietnam. They were intended for breeding, but the villagers found that they consumed more food than five or six Vietnamese families did. "So they ate 'em," Benton said. Another village chief demanded air conditioners even though his village had no electricity. Benton threw up his hands and ordered air conditioners.

The village aid program was bound to fail because all that most Vietnamese wanted was to own some land and to farm it in peace. So American policy began to work at cross purposes—while American advisers tried to help the Vietnamese improve their lives, American bombers destroyed their villages and made life miserable. Winning hearts and minds in South Vietnam could not be done while American soldiers were fighting a war in the same country.

CHAPTER EIGHT

In Country

I landed in this country,
One year of life to give,
My only friend, a weapon,
My only prayer, to live.

I walked away from freedom
And the life that I had known,
I passed the weary faces
Of the others going home.

Boonie Rats, Boonie Rats,
Scared but not alone,
300 days more or less
Then I'm going home.

—Soldier's song, 1970

WHO fought in Vietnam? To supply the huge troop build-up, men were drafted—called into military service by law. During the war, 2,215,000 men were drafted. Another 8,720,000 men and women signed up voluntarily—many for patriotic reasons, others because they expected to be drafted soon anyway and wanted to choose their branch of service.

The draft system was unpopular and unfair. Men could legally avoid the draft by enrolling in college. Thus, the greatest burden fell on those who were too poor to afford a college education. Furthermore, as the need for soldiers increased, younger and younger men were drafted. The average age of an American soldier in Vietnam was nineteen, as compared with age twenty-six for soldiers in World War II.

On his eighteenth birthday, every American man had thirty days to register for the draft. After registering, he could be called up at any time. The teenage American knew his turn had come when he got the letter from his local draft board that began: "Greetings." Nearly all of those who were drafted went into the army.

A new soldier went through basic training in the United States for eight weeks. Once his orders came for assignment to Vietnam, he usually had a few days to say goodbye to his family and friends. After that, he was on a plane or a ship headed for Vietnam.

To some, Vietnam was like an alien planet—the sights and sounds were totally foreign to young men raised in the world's most prosperous country. The first things that hit them were the heat and the smell. The temperature in South Vietnam often climbed over 100, and the humidity was always high. Vietnam had no sewage system to dispose of human wastes. Each day, the base latrines (toilets) were emptied and the contents burned with fuel oil. The odor hung in the air constantly.

The newly arrived soldier was now "in country," as Americans called their time in Vietnam. At the airfield, a bus was waiting to take the soldiers to their barracks. The windows of the bus were covered with wire mesh to keep out grenades. For the next year, no matter where he was stationed, the young American lived in constant danger.

The bus passed Vietnamese shantytowns whose people worked on the base. The job of garbage collection was a prized one, for American garbage was a treasure trove for poor Vietnamese. A second look at the shanties showed that the roofs and walls were covered with flattened beer and soda cans. (Americans in the field soon learned to flatten the cans themselves, for an empty can could be used as a grenade casing by the Viet Cong.)

Wherever Americans went, little children clustered around, calling them "number one" and asking for gum, cigarettes, or money. If they were turned down, the children responded with a cry of "number ten"—the worst, unluckiest number to a Vietnamese. To some Americans, it was shocking to learn that most Vietnamese were so poor they could be paid to do almost anything.

Americans came to feel that there was another, more sinister, reason for Vietnamese helpfulness. Viet Cong attackers usually knew exactly where ammunition dumps and other important targets were located. They could have learned this only from the Vietnamese civilians who moved freely in and out of the bases.

A newly arrived soldier had to wait at the barracks for a few days before he learned his destination. After the first large American units arrived in country, replacements were sent in individually to fill in for those who had been killed or wounded.

This method of replacement often hurt troop morale. In previous wars, units trained together; they knew and trusted each other by the time they went into battle. In Vietnam, it took time for a new man to be accepted by his comrades. For one thing, his very inexperience made him a danger to those who fought with him. For another, men whose buddies had been killed or maimed tried not to get close to others.

Before long, the "new guy" found himself on a search-and-destroy mission. Helicopters ferried troops to a target area, where their first task was to set up a fire-support base. They immediately established a perimeter—the defensive line that protected a unit of any size. The first grunts to arrive spread out to serve as a "human" perimeter, taking their places around the line to keep the enemy away while the base was being built. Then the perimeter was strengthened with barbed wire, sand bags, mine fields, and trenches.

Huge transport helicopters brought in bulldozers, building supplies, and finally the artillery guns that would protect troops in the field. Since a fire base was usually isolated—like a miniature Dien Bien Phu—it had to get all its supplies by air.

From the fire base, troops stalked the enemy. They called this "hump-

A Viet Cong soldier crouches in a bunker. (Courtesy of U.S. Army)

ing the boonies.'' Americans were in unfamiliar territory, searching for forces who knew the area well. Sometimes they would march all day and find nothing—a ''walk in the sun.'' Even that was exhausting. The men hacked new paths through jungle growth and elephant grass. (Old paths were usually booby-trapped.) On his first march, a soldier soon drank up all the water he had brought in his canteen. With experience, he learned to carry several canteens of fresh water, often flavored with Kool-Aid.

The scariest job on these patrols was walking ''point.'' The point man went first, usually some yards ahead of the main force. He was, in effect, supposed to take the first fire from the enemy, alerting those who followed.

The search-and-destroy tactic let the enemy decide whether to fight. Viet Cong could hide in tall grass or trees as a platoon of Americans marched by. If the odds favored them, they attacked; if not, they did not reveal their presence.

Thus, the enemy could choose the best position for an attack, dig in, and wait for a group of Americans to approach. The VC used many forms of camouflage. They hid in the tops of trees, in rice-paddy dikes, even in giant anthills. The shovel was an important piece of equipment. With it, a VC could dig himself a spider hole, out of which he popped without warning, armed with anything from a machine gun to a grenade launcher.

Fear of hidden enemies caused American troops to fire at any movement or sound. This meant that they used tremendous amounts of ammunition. The grunt's standard weapon was the M-16 rifle, which could fire either single shots or on full automatic, like a machine gun. The troops called full automatic fire ''rock-and-roll.'' A ''new guy'' was especially edgy, and his first response to an enemy attack was to let fly with his full clip of twenty bullets. Then he would be defenseless until he inserted another clip. And there was a limit to the number of clips a soldier could carry on patrol. Green troops quickly used all they had, and then had to rely on machetes or trench shovels to defend themselves.

Because a firefight usually began as an ambush, the battle was confusing and terrifying. The first shot often set off a fusillade of wild firing. In the jungle, it was usually impossible to tell where the attack was coming from. Only with experience did soldiers learn to regroup and form a perimeter to defend themselves.

When the bait had been taken and the enemy attacked, the American officer in charge radioed to the fire base for help. Giving his position, he would call for an artillery barrage from the fire base. After the shells began to fall, the radio man would direct them closer to the enemy position.

Mistakes in the coordinates sometimes caused Americans to take "friendly fire"—be shelled by their own artillery.

Helicopter gunships and reinforcements soon arrived on the scene. If they could see the ground below, they fired at the enemy. If not, the radio man had to tell them where to shoot. A landing zone had to be prepared, and defended, to allow the medevacs to take the wounded off the battlefield. The VC expected these too, and pilots on such a mission knew the LZ would be a hot one. They and their crews were sitting ducks while they tried to get the wounded aboard.

After a battle ended, the dead were zippered into rubber body bags for the medevacs to take away. But when soldiers had stepped on land mines or been hit by artillery, there was little left to put into the bag.

A particularly dangerous mission was the "lurp"—long-range reconnaissance patrol—on which soldiers roamed far from their fire base and stayed in the field for days. Their officers knew that to set up an overnight camp in daylight would invite an attack that night. Enemy eyes were always watching. So a field officer would look for an easily defended site

An army medic helps a wounded soldier on the battlefield. Regular soldiers were trained to treat each other's wounds when no medic was available—one reason why the percentage of wounded men who survived in Vietnam was higher than in any previous American war. (The Bettmann Archive)

during the day's march and take his men back to it after dark. They set up a defensive perimeter and dug foxholes as deep as possible. Afterward, they ate a meal of C-rations—canned food—washed down with grape Kool-Aid. Those who were not on sentry duty tried to get some sleep.

Sentries on night patrol felt particularly threatened. The sounds of jungle animals and insects were magnified in the imagination into VC troops creeping closer. No one really knew what was in the darkness beyond the perimeter, and Americans took to calling the VC the "ghosts." Soldiers on night sentry duty would whisper to the next man: "The ghosts are out there."

Sometimes the ghosts were not imaginary. The sentry would scream "Incoming!" as he heard the first enemy artillery shells whistling through the air. Night attacks were a scene of total confusion. Men woke, rifles in hand, and began to fire instinctively toward the perimeter without waiting to be sure if the enemy was charging it. The rattle of machine guns and the shrieks of the wounded drowned out shouted commands. Once again, "Charlie" (from "Victor Charles," the radio code words for VC) had picked his own time and place to attack.

At night, machine gunners used strings of tracer bullets, in which every sixth bullet was coated with a chemical that made it glow when fired. American bullets glowed orange; enemy tracers left a green trail. Tracers made it easier to tell where the bullets were going—and had the added effect of blowing up any gasoline tanks or ammunition dumps they hit. Like strings of deadly fireworks, the tracers passed back and forth.

American aircraft called to the scene rained down rocket fire and their own machine-gun tracers. A low-flying gunship—called Puff the Magic Dragon by the troops—could fire 6,000 bullets a minute from its multi-barreled machine guns. Shells of white phosphorus ("Willie Peter") were dropped to light up the area so that the enemy could be seen. To some, the night fights had an eerie beauty, but they were best appreciated from a distance.

Americans often greeted the dawn with a "mad minute"—a general firing of every available weapon. It was directed aimlessly against the forests around the camp, where the enemy might (or might not) be waiting. It was an expression of frustration, of fear, and of anger. The enemy would not fight fair—that was how he had survived against the Chinese, the Mongols, and the French. He attacked when he was strong and hid when he was weak.

Back home, the government told the American troops they were going to Vietnam as saviors. So it was a great shock for these troops to arrive in

A nighttime firefight was a scene of eerie beauty. Here, helicopter machine gunners fire strings of glowing tracer bullets at suspected enemy movement outside the perimeter of a base. Ground forces inside the base fire from their bunkers. (Courtesy of U.S. Army)

Vietnam and realize that many villagers saw *them* as the enemy. As one American wrote in a letter home: "To see your buddy step on a VC anti-personnel mine is a hard thing to take, but the real scare is when you go back to your base camp and see the smiling villagers all around you and then start to wonder if one of them set it there."

It was common for Americans on patrol to be fired on from a village. But when they entered the village, they would find only women, children, and old men. "No VC! No VC!" the villagers would shout, using some of the few English words they knew. A search of the village often unearthed weapons, supplies, and other evidence that it was indeed a VC stronghold. Sometimes Viet Cong soldiers themselves would be found in tunnels under the village.

John Muir, a marine in Vietnam in 1966, described one village his unit found:

> [There was] a little old lady and a little old man and two very small children. According to them, the rest of the family has been spirited away, either by the ARVN or by the VC—they'd either been drafted into one army or the other. So there's only four of them and they have a pot of rice that's big enough to feed fifty people. And rice, once it's cooked, will not keep. They gotta be feeding the VC. So [we] set the house on fire and the roof started cooking off ammunition because all through the thatch they had ammunition stored.

The Americans tried to clear VC-held areas by moving all the villagers

out and then declaring the area a "free-fire zone." Anyone still there was regarded as an enemy and could be fired on at will. Combined with the New Life hamlet policy, this practice destroyed village life in much of South Vietnam. By 1968, one third of the villagers had been uprooted from their homes.

Villagers and suspected Viet Cong were taken prisoner and questioned. If they did not answer—often because they spoke no English—they were sometimes tortured or killed. A favorite method was to take several prisoners up in a helicopter. The first one who refused to answer questions was thrown out. Usually, the remaining prisoners were more cooperative.

Nowhere in Vietnam was an American soldier truly safe. At any time, the VC could announce its presence by lobbing a mortar shell into an American camp. In the cities, the VC planted bombs. Sometimes they filled the hollow frame of a bicycle with explosives and parked it outside a bar full of American troops.

Young children would be used to set off grenades among unsuspecting groups of Americans. "Coca-Cola girls" approached the soldiers selling soft drinks or food. Sometimes these were poisoned. Many American soldiers came to regard all Vietnamese as the enemy. Americans began to treat the villagers with greater brutality, losing their support and becoming more like an army sent to conquer a hostile country.

When the American troop build-up began in 1965, the basic weapon of the U.S. soldier was changed from the M-14 rifle to the M-16. The M-16 was lighter and easier to carry. But soldiers found that the M-16 often jammed, leaving them defenseless in the middle of a fight. Because of its design, the rifle had to be kept unusually clean—which was impossible in the mud and rain of Vietnam. Even a soldier's sweat could jam the weapon.

In 1967, a marine wrote a letter to Congress saying that during a recent fight, "practically every one of our dead was found with his rifle torn down [disassembled] next to him where he was trying to fix it." Congress demanded that the Department of Defense turn the M-16 into a better weapon, and eventually it was, but soldiers were still leery of it.

Two American soldiers drag a Viet Cong prisoner from a bunker in the background. Many VC soldiers were ragged and poorly equipped. (The Bettmann Archive)

At least one man in each patrol also carried an M-60 machine gun. Other soldiers lugged strings of ammunition to supply the machine gunners. Those who fired the M-60s discovered—often too late—that the enemy forces tried to kill the machine gunners first.

Another member of the patrol carried an M-79 grenade launcher. The M-79 could fire a grenade up to 300 yards—the length of three football fields. Each soldier also had a supply of hand grenades. The M-26 fragmentation grenade exploded into deadly shards of flying metal. Other grenades contained tear gas or smoke to mark a unit's location for the helicopters. Phosphorus grenades scattered burning fragments that cut through uniforms and embedded themselves in human flesh.

Larger units carried howitzers and other hand-held artillery. Among the shells they could fire were "beehives," which contained 8,500 small steel arrows that sounded like a swarm of bees when they went off. They were devastating when fired against enemy troops charging a perimeter.

Claymore mines, set on the ground, sent a deadly spray of pellets in the direction the mine was placed. They could be set off electronically and were often used around the perimeter of a base. Their force was equal to about seventy shotguns going off at once. Similar to these were cluster bombs, which were dropped from planes and sprayed out hundreds of metal balls when they exploded.

One of the most controversial weapons was napalm—a jellied form of gasoline. Napalm bombs exploded when they hit the ground, spraying flaming droplets that stuck to anything—or anyone—they hit.

The standard weapon of the North Vietnamese Army was the Russian AK-47 rifle. Though it was less accurate and had a shorter effective range than the M-16, it was simpler and more reliable. It could be easily broken down for cleaning, and it seldom jammed in combat.

The VC and the NVA had machine guns that they used with devastating results when they attacked unwary search-and-destroy patrols. When attacking bases, the NVA used portable rocket launchers. Its troops also used light mortar guns designed to be broken up into three pieces so that each member of the trio assigned to fight together could carry one of the parts.

At first, the Viet Cong's weapons were old and inferior to the weapons that Americans supplied to the South Vietnamese army. But the VC stole American weapons—from dead soldiers and from supply bases—and

These soldiers are getting ready to search for and disarm Viet Cong booby traps. They have wrapped discarded flak jackets (bulletproof vests) around their heads and bodies as protection against flying shrapnel. (AP/Wide World)

also used homemade weapons to great advantage. Among these was the bangalore torpedo, a bamboo tube filled with explosives. Sappers used the torpedoes to blast apart the barbed-wire defenses around a camp's perimeter.

The most feared weapons of the Viet Cong were their hidden booby traps and mines. The unlucky point man on an American patrol might be the first to trigger one of these. Hidden trip wires in the jungle could set off anything from a captured claymore mine to a crude bow and arrow hidden at stomach level. About 11 percent of all American deaths in Vietnam were caused by booby traps set by an enemy who had long gone elsewhere.

The VC booby traps were designed to be as horrible as possible in order to destroy morale. The most famous were the punji sticks, usually dipped in human excrement and sharp enough to pierce the boot of an unwary grunt.

Even more frightening was the "Bouncing Betty," a mine that was set off by a hidden trip wire. When triggered, the Bouncing Betty popped into the air, about waist high, before exploding. The man who triggered it was usually cut in half. Though the Bouncing Betty was devised by the American CIA, the VC stole so many of them that American soldiers regarded it as one of the enemy's most deadly weapons.

Soldiers got a welcome break from combat when they were given "R and R"—rest and recreation. They were allowed one week outside Vietnam at least once during their tour of duty, but usually they flew to American bases within Vietnam. They found conditions here sharply different from those in the countryside.

At An Khe (pronounced Ahn Kay), in the highlands, the army built a recreation area called Disneyland East. Helicopters from American ships flew in beer, ice, and ice cream. The air conditioning in some officers' clubs was so strong that fireplaces were necessary. On the bases, Americans could spend their money in the PX (post exchange) to buy stereos, food, clothing, and many other things they might enjoy back home.

On these "vacations" from the war, soldiers could sleep in real beds, drink in air-conditioned bars, go to nightclubs where bands played the latest hit songs from the United States, and gorge themselves on rich food in French restaurants. They could spend the day sailing and surfing at the beach or swimming in the base's pool. They brooded over the fact that for many American soldiers in Vietnam—the supply troops, the commanding officers and their staffs—this was daily life.

Out in the countryside, pleasures were fewer but just as welcome. MACV tried to keep up the men's morale by making life as comfortable as possible. The military newspaper *Stars and Stripes* carried news of home and of battles within Vietnam. MACV ran a radio and a television station that gave the weather for many hometowns in the States. Soldiers carried transistor radios wherever they went in Vietnam, and the sounds of the Beatles and the Rolling Stones provided background music for the war.

Chaplains held religious services in the combat areas and gave last rites to the dying and dead, often risking their own lives to do so. The USO (United Service Organizations) sent American entertainers to cheer the troops. Comedian Bob Hope, who had entertained troops in World War II and Korea, went to Vietnam as well. Hope brought along beautiful dancers and singers, who were a good tonic for war-weary soldiers.

Slack times in the fighting gave the men time to think, and what they thought about most was home. When they heard the sound of incoming Hueys, they gathered around. The helicopters brought birthday and Christmas presents—even cookies and cakes. Most of all, soldiers hoped for a letter from a loved one back home. Captain Rodney Chastant described what the letters meant:

> Mom, I appreciate all your letters. . . . I'm eager to read anything about what you are doing or the family is doing. . . . For a while, as I read your letters, I am a normal person. I'm not killing people, or worried about being killed. While I read your letters, I'm not carrying guns or grenades. Instead I am going ice skating with David [his brother] or walking through a department store to exchange a lamp shade. It is great to know your family's safe, living in a secure country; a country made secure by thousands upon thousands of men who have died for that country.

Captain Chastant signed up to extend his tour of duty an additional six months. He was killed before completing it, aged twenty-five.

Women went to Vietnam also, both as military personnel and as civilians. Women in the army, the navy, and the air force served as mapmakers, decoders, air traffic controllers, photographers, and translators. Many were clerks in the military base headquarters.

Religious groups sent nuns and lay women to work in schools, hospitals, and the orphanages that sheltered the thousands of children made homeless by the fighting. Most civilian women worked for the Red Cross, sometimes as "Donut Dollies" who ran canteens and clubs in the base areas. Others were coptered to combat areas to raise the troops' morale. Just the sight of an American woman was another reminder of the World that the soldiers hoped to return to. The Donut Dollies played cards, pool, and Ping-Pong with the soldiers. They organized sing-alongs and art shows and modeled the latest fashions—which in the sixties included mini-skirts and hot pants.

The most important—and dangerous—role played by American women in Vietnam was that of nurse. No experience in a civilian hospital could prepare a nurse for the kinds of wounds she saw in Vietnam. Many soldiers' arms and legs were blown off, or their bodies were riddled with fragmentation grenade shards. Some were blinded or bore wounds that scarred them terribly. Helicopter pilots who had crashed often had burns over much of their bodies. The nurses also had to treat men with malaria, bubonic plague, and other diseases that they had never seen before.

One nurse remembered thinking, " 'You work in it for a while, you'll get more accustomed to it, and it won't be so shocking.' But you never did because every boy that came in was an individual. You knew that he had a mother and a father, a girlfriend and boyfriend.''

Many nurses worked in the big, fully equipped hospitals in base areas and on ships offshore. Others served in the field hospitals set up in tents on the edges of combat zones. When a medevac arrived at a field hospital

Donut Dollies—as American Red Cross workers were sometimes called—ran canteens and clubs in base areas. Here, a Donut Dolly braces herself as a group of tired, muddy paratroopers returns from combat. (Army News Features)

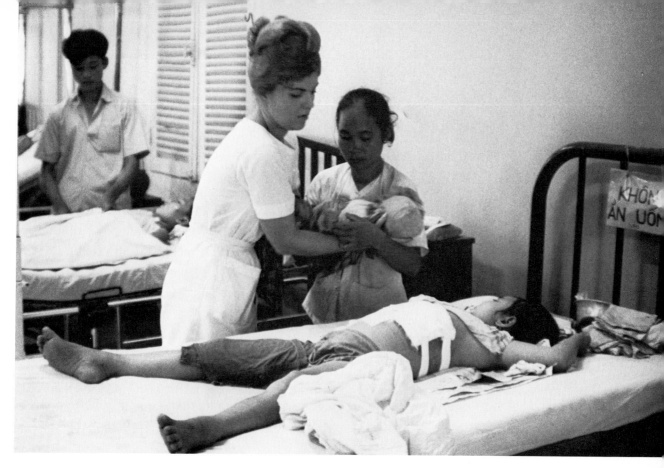

with freshly wounded men, the nurses' first task was sometimes the hard-est—triage. "Triage" was to divide the wounded into three groups: those who could survive without immediate care, those who needed immediate care, and those who could not survive. This decision had to be made be-cause there were only so many nurses and doctors. When casualties were high, they often worked around the clock. Someone—usually the first nurse to see the wounded—had to decide, in effect, which men to try to save and which to let die.

Like the soldiers, nurses knew they were always vulnerable to enemy attacks. The men, at least, could fight back. All the nurses could do was treat the wounded, pray that they would live, and then watch as some died despite all their efforts. As combat nurse Judy Jenkins remembered:

At a hospital in South Viet-nam, a U.S. nurse takes a seriously wounded baby from the arms of its mother as an-other child lies bandaged on a hospital bed. These chil-dren were among those wounded in the bombing of a hamlet in the Mekong Delta. American soldiers donated blood to help save their lives. (The Bettmann Archive)

> The knowledge . . . that everywhere was a combat zone was a hard thing
> to live with. Day in and day out. The war was with you all the time. . . . I
> remember feeling the little tinkle of dog tags around my neck and reminding
> myself I could go home in a body bag. . . . Yeah, Vietnam had a way of
> playing on your mind.

Those soldiers who reached the end of their year's tour of duty without being killed or wounded could now go home. For most, the only feeling was relief. Some were proud of having served their country. Others were haunted with a sense of failure. They had searched for an enemy who remained elusive and undefeated. They had swept through territory without taking it from the Viet Cong. They had seen their buddies die alongside them. They had answered their country's call to battle and fought bravely. But they had not seen victory, and they went home with no feeling of success or triumph. As Philip Caputo, a departing marine, wrote:

> We stood waiting in the sun at the edge of the runway . . . and we watched [as new replacements] filed off the big transport plane. . . . I felt sorry for [them], knowing that they would all grow old in this land of endless dying. . . .
>
> None of them looked at us. They marched away. Shouldering our sea-bags, we climbed up the ramp into the plane, the plane we had all dreamed about, the grand, mythological Freedom Bird. A joyous shout went up. . . . Below lay the rice paddies and the green, folded hills where we had lost our friends and our youth. . . .
>
> None of us was a hero. We had survived, and that was our only victory.

CHAPTER NINE

The War at Home

Where have all the flowers gone?
Long time passing. . . .
Where have all the soldiers gone?
Long time passing. . . .
They've gone to graveyards, every one.
Oh, when will they ever learn?

—Lyrics from a song by Pete Seeger

THE soldier returning from Vietnam came home to a country where another war was going on. Instead of receiving the welcome of a grateful nation, the Vietnam vets saw parades of Americans who opposed the war. The Vietnam War was a battle for hearts and minds in the United States as well as in Southeast Asia.

The decade of the 1960s began on a high note of idealism. John F. Kennedy's inaugural speech made Americans feel they had a mission to defend freedom all over the world. Kennedy's words appealed most to the "baby-boom" generation—those young Americans who had been born in huge numbers since World War II. Still children when Kennedy was elected, the baby boomers grew up during the most prosperous time in American history. Millions of their parents had bought television sets and homes in new suburbs. The baby-boom children, growing up in comfort and security, yearned for a challenge.

One of their first challenges was the civil rights movement. The struggle of American blacks to win their full rights as citizens had begun to make front-page news in the late 1950s. Young Americans became aware that in many places in the United States, blacks were not allowed to vote, go to school with whites, eat in white restaurants, sit with whites in theaters, or use the same public bathrooms and drinking fountains.

Americans watched the civil rights struggle on their TV sets. They saw Southern police officers use dogs, clubs, and cattle prods against black

Americans who were peacefully marching to demand their rights. Such scenes made many baby boomers realize that not everyone enjoyed the secure life of the suburbs, in which the police were respected friends. What they saw made them more willing to question and challenge authority.

Besides protest marches, civil rights workers pioneered the use of "sit-ins," in which they refused to leave restaurants until they were served. Their success showed that Americans could take direct action to improve society. Whites as well as blacks went south to join the civil rights movement. It was a training ground for many who would later march against the Vietnam War.

Despite the cost in money and lives, wars have usually brought forth Americans' deepest feelings of patriotism and pride. Since the Civil War, Americans had rallied around their government whenever the nation went to war. That changed in the 1960s as many Americans marched in the streets to oppose our presence in Vietnam.

The antiwar movement grew gradually. When President Kennedy was elected in 1960, most Americans had still never heard of Vietnam. Very few people opposed Kennedy's decision to send more advisers there.

In 1963, doubts began to grow among American journalists assigned to cover Vietnam. American newspapers and magazines backed Kennedy's anti-Communist policy, and their reporters did not question our involvement. But those who went into the countryside saw that Diem did not have the support of his people. Some American military advisers privately told the journalists that Diem's army did not perform well in combat.

MACV headquarters in Saigon continued to declare that the war would soon be won. At late afternoon press conferences, a MACV officer would describe Diem's successes to the assembled reporters. The reporters, who could see with their own eyes that Diem's hold on the country was weak, began to call the press conferences "the five o'clock follies."

Reporters' doubts seldom made their way into print. Many of their editors in the United States felt that it was unpatriotic to oppose the government's policy in Vietnam. In 1963, when *The New York Times* printed a critical story by reporter David Halberstam, President Kennedy hinted to the *Times*'s publisher that Halberstam should be replaced. The publisher resisted Kennedy's suggestion, but in the early years few other newspapers were so courageous. Only after the Buddhist suicides made front-page news did Americans start to question our support of the South Vietnamese government.

When President Johnson sent combat troops to Vietnam in 1965, the war became a more important issue to Americans. They had voted for Johnson as the peace candidate, and when the huge troop build-up began only months after his election, many people felt he had lied to them. When American soldiers began to come back to their families in body bags, people started to realize that we had, almost without public debate, gotten into a major war.

Year after year, the government issued reports to show we were winning the war. Yet the war dragged on. Critics of the government's policy proved that some of the reports were false. Americans began to have the uneasy feeling that they could not trust their leaders to tell the truth. The contrast between what the government said and what was actually happening became known as the credibility gap.

Americans were willing to fight communism. But they were troubled when Communists seemed to be poor people in farming villages. Pictures of children burned by U.S. napalm strikes touched the consciences of Americans. United States bombers continued to pound North Vietnam and parts of South Vietnam as well. Yet the Vietnamese would not give up, and Americans wondered why. Some people said it was wrong for the world's most powerful nation to be bombing a backward country that posed no direct threat to the United States.

Secretary of State Dean Rusk accused critics of the bombing of having a double standard. Rusk said: "A bomb carried by a boy on a bicycle or mortar shells fired at the Da Nang base . . . are just as much bombs as those carried by planes to the North." What Rusk could not see was that there was something wrong with the idea of fighting boys on bicycles with gigantic jet bombers. But ordinary Americans *could* see that—every night on television.

The Vietnam War was called the first televised war. Since the last American war, in Korea, nearly every household in the United States had acquired a television set. TV now brought the news to more Americans than newspapers or magazines did. Every night at dinnertime, American families could watch what they were paying for 9,000 miles away. War is always ugly, and few Americans liked what they saw.

In 1965, viewers saw marines using their cigarette lighters to set fire to some grass huts in a Vietnamese village. In a shaking voice, CBS News reporter Morley Safer described what was happening on the scene. An American officer said he had orders to burn the village because enemy fire had come from there. However, the camera turned to show a crowd of weeping women holding babies and watching their homes burn. "If there were Viet Cong in the hamlet," Safer said, "they were long gone. . . . The day's operation burned down one hundred fifty houses, wounded three women, killed one baby, wounded one marine, and netted four prisoners—four old men who could not answer questions put to them in English. Four old men who had no idea what an I.D. card was."

The burning of the village, said Safer, was "the frustration of Vietnam in miniature. American firepower can win a victory here. But to a Vietnamese peasant whose home means a lifetime of back-breaking labor, it will take more than presidential promises to convince him that we are on his side."

Television brought home the reality of war. The sight of maimed children, homeless villagers, and bombed farmland told the story like no newspaper article could. Americans saw what their soldiers already knew—that our enemy included women and children, poor farmers whose homes we were destroying. These were not faceless Communist demons. They were ordinary people.

Students had a particular interest in the war because it was their generation that was fighting and dying in Vietnam. They wanted to know what the war was all about, and it became a much discussed subject on college campuses. After the first American combat troops were sent to Vietnam in March 1965, the first "teach-in" was held at the University of Michigan. Named after the sit-ins of the civil rights movement, a teach-in was a public discussion of the issues of the war.

Americans knew little about Vietnam's history. Many thought, for example, that it had always been two countries, or that the French had first come to Vietnam after World War II. Teach-ins spread to other colleges around the country, and students began to realize that the issues in Vietnam were more complicated than communism versus democracy.

Students had learned from the civil rights movement that when you saw injustice, you fought it in public. The first antiwar march took place in Washington in April 1965. Led by the Students for a Democratic Society (SDS), it drew about 25,000 people. The marchers sang "We Shall Overcome," the civil rights anthem that took on new meaning in the years of antiwar protest. In later years, the country would see marches ten times as large as that first one.

Other, more direct, protests began. In August 1965, students gathered around the Oakland Army Terminal in California, where American soldiers were sent to Vietnam. The students tried unsuccessfully to block the troop trains. They passed antiwar leaflets to the soldiers through the train windows and carried banners reading, "You haven't killed yet—don't!"

An enraged University of Wisconsin student screams at a police officer after Madison police used riot clubs and tear gas against students protesting the war. (The Bettmann Archive)

In October 1965, in New York City, a young man named David J. Miller publicly burned his draft card on the steps of the building where draftees reported. The draft card had to be carried by all American men to show that they had registered for the draft. It was against the law to destroy the card, but many others followed Miller's example in the years of the war. The card burners were risking arrest to show in a very public way that they opposed the policies of their own government. Miller himself spent two years in jail for his action.

As the student protests grew, some Americans accused the protesters of encouraging the enemy to continue the fight. Instead of bringing the war to an end, they were only prolonging it.

Protesters would respond: What are you supposed to do when your country is fighting an unjust war? When you vote for a peace candidate who wages war? When your government is calling you to die for a cause you believe is wrong?

The student protests were part of a lifestyle of rebellion, with its own values and its own vocabulary. "Hippies" showed their opposition to authority by letting their hair grow, wearing love beads, and smoking marijuana. Young Americans by the millions imitated them. Some tried other "mind-expanding" drugs such as LSD, and "dropped out"—of college, of society in general—to live in hippie communities such as Haight-Ashbury in San Francisco and the East Village in New York City.

"Underground" newspapers appeared in many cities, spreading the views of the counterculture—those who opposed traditional American values. "Psychedelic" art, such as the posters of Peter Max, stood for the new, freer vision of life that the baby boomers developed for themselves. Gurus, or religious teachers from India, attracted followers among young Americans.

Antiwar marchers began to sing protest songs when they gathered. Bob Dylan, Phil Ochs, Pete Seeger, and others composed songs that declared "the times, they are a-changin'." In Dylan's words, "Something is happening here, but you don't know what it is—do you, Mr. Jones?" Dylan's young fans felt that they were different from any generation that had come before. Antiwar protests united them in a rebellion against the older generation, and the differences in thought and lifestyle between young people and older Americans became known as the generation gap.

Pro-war Americans believed that antiwar protesters were making the war last longer by encouraging the enemy to continue the fight. Some staged marches in support of the war, like this one in St. Louis, Missouri. (The Bettmann Archive)

Many parents of the rebellious baby boomers were angered and disturbed by the antiwar protests. The older generation had fought World War II to defend the world against Japanese and Nazi aggression. Most felt that the Vietnam War was a war against Communist aggression. They disapproved of their sons' and daughters' marching in the streets against the war—and of their different lifestyles. Families became bitterly divided over the war.

The older generation believed, as reporter Malcolm Browne wrote from Vietnam with sadness:

> In our minds' eyes we are always the good guys. . . . We send forth our young men in uniform to destroy the enemies of our way of life and to keep the world good. Never, in our minds' eyes, could we be guilty of needlessly killing innocents; of torturing prisoners; of being ungallant to women; of cowardice; of making the poor people of another nation poorer still.

Yet slowly, more Americans were beginning to see all these things happen in Vietnam. Even the older generation began to feel that something had to be done about the war. As some said, "Win it, or get out."

By 1966, the bombing of the North, which was intended to end the war quickly, had been going on for nearly two years. Ho Chi Minh continued to refuse offers of peace talks. The "carrot and stick" approach had not worked. So Senator William Fulbright, the head of the Senate Foreign Relations Committee, decided to hold hearings on the war. Fulbright had helped to guide the Gulf of Tonkin Resolution through Congress, but he felt betrayed because he had not seen it justifying an all-out war. He was troubled by the growing lists of American wounded and dead.

Fulbright invited both critics of the war and President Johnson's officials to testify before his committee. As Americans watched the televised hearings, they saw that their leaders were now divided into two groups— the "hawks" and the "doves." The hawks wanted to press the war to victory. The doves opposed the war and sought some way to withdraw American forces.

Committee members who were doves were critical of the American war effort. Some administration officials accused them of bringing "good news to Hanoi," repeating the charge that any American who opposed the war was in fact supporting the enemy.

That set the tone for the angry debate that followed. Senator Fulbright told Secretary of State Rusk, "Vietnam is their country. It is not our country."

Rusk snapped back, "South Vietnam is not Hanoi's country."

And Fulbright pointed out, "It used to be one country."

Few Americans knew this, because three presidents had told them that the North was invading the South. This was the kind of information that students had been learning in teach-ins. Now other Americans were beginning to find out what Vietnam was all about.

Senator George McGovern was one of the leaders of the doves. He pointed out that nearly all of South Vietnam's generals had fought on the side of the French during the war that ended with Dien Bien Phu. McGovern compared them to Benedict Arnold, the traitor of the American Revolution, and asked how the South Vietnamese could be expected to support them. Had the United States in fact taken over the French role in denying the Vietnamese the right to govern themselves?

Senator George Aiken of Vermont said, only half jokingly, that we should "simply announce that the United States has won the war and then withdraw [its] troops from Vietnam."

In February 1967, Dr. Martin Luther King, Jr., the leader of the civil rights movement, added his voice to those who publicly opposed the war. This was a blow to President Johnson, who had strongly backed the civil rights movement and expected King's support in return. However, Johnson's War on Poverty was costly and had taken second place to the expense of fighting the Vietnam War. King declared, "The promises of the Great Society have been shot down on the battlefield of Vietnam."

During the summer of 1967, riots broke out in black ghettoes in Detroit, Michigan, Newark, New Jersey, and other cities. In Detroit, the violence was so intense that the U.S. Army had to be called in. Though these riots were outbursts of frustration against poverty and prejudice, they set a new tone for the antiwar movement as well. Americans began to wonder whether fighting communism 9,000 miles away in Vietnam was as important as solving the problems of poverty and prejudice at home.

Some radical antiwar groups turned completely against the American system of government. They planted bombs in government buildings and committed other acts of violence. Some carried Viet Cong flags in protest marches, burned the American flag, and chanted, ''Ho, Ho, Ho Chi Minh, the NLF is gonna win!'' These tactics only aroused fear and anger among the majority of people. Though many Americans questioned the war, they were not about to revolt against society as a whole.

The draft became a focus for protest. Marchers shouted slogans such as ''Hell no, we won't go!'' Antiwar organizations helped those who were likely to be drafted escape to Canada, Sweden, and other countries that would shelter them. Pamphlets gave advice on how to avoid serving in the military. Young men compared notes on how to appear physically or mentally unfit to the draft board doctors.

October 21, 1967. Military police, bayonets ready, confront thousands of jeering protesters at an antiwar demonstration in front of the Pentagon. (The Bettmann Archive)

DOUBLESPEAK

Terms such as "body bags" and "body counts" seemed cold and mechanical efforts to hide the pain and suffering of the war. The American military command at MACV became skilled in the art of "doublespeak," issuing lists of "correct" terms for officers to use in their reports. Search-and-destroy missions were renamed "search-and-clear operations." The enemy's surprise tactics were called "ambushes," but Americans did not ambush the VC—they "engaged them on all sides." Our soldiers did not step on VC booby traps—they "encountered automatic ambushes." When American troops withdrew from an area, they did not retreat—they were "redeployed." Killing Viet Cong became known as "pacification."

In Vietnam, American soldiers who had chosen to serve their country were disturbed by the protesters and draft resisters. Some of them sent letters to newspapers, explaining why they supported the war. Robert Feltzer, a twenty-two-year-old marine, wrote his hometown paper:

> I wonder if [the antiwar protesters] have ever been scared. I have been scared and still am scared. . . . But I know it has got to be done and I do it. Maybe if they came over here and saw guys blown up by mines, getting hit by mortars or being shot, maybe then it would sink into their thick skulls what we are doing here to keep them free so they can go to college.

Feltzer died six months into his tour of duty in Vietnam. He, and those like him who returned home in rubber body bags, added another, silent protest. Americans saw more and more of their sons and neighbors being killed in a distant land, and they were troubled. The body count on the TV news each night showed that we were winning the war, but we seemed no closer to victory.

On October 21, 1967, thousands of Americans gathered in Washington, D.C., for another protest march. They surrounded the Pentagon—the headquarters of the Department of Defense in nearby Arlington, Virginia—in an effort to block anyone from leaving. Many of the most outlandish members of the counterculture were there. Some chanted a "mantra" of an Eastern religion in an effort to make the Pentagon building rise into the air. "Flower children" stuck flowers into the barrels of rifles held by soldiers guarding the building. They were trying to show that the power of peace was stronger than guns or bullets.

Later that day, a crowd gathered at the Lincoln Memorial. The peace movement had grown far beyond a few angry students. The marchers now included Vietnam veterans, movie stars, doctors, lawyers, union members, priests, ministers, rabbis, and nuns. One speaker said, "The enemy, we believe, is Lyndon Johnson, whom we elected as a peace candidate and who betrayed us within three months." Many in the crowd chanted one of the antiwar movement's cruelest slogans: "Hey, hey, LBJ, how many kids did you kill today?"

Johnson was expected to run for reelection the following year. Some antiwar Democrats—members of his own party—looked for a candidate to oppose him, and Minnesota Senator Eugene McCarthy offered himself. The peace marchers now had someone to rally around, and they began to volunteer for McCarthy's campaign. Knowing that older Americans distrusted hippies, their motto became "Get clean for Gene." They cut their hair and discarded their jeans for suits and dresses—to convince the older generation that they were "regular" Americans.

Johnson also wanted to reassure Americans. He brought General Westmoreland back from Vietnam to give a series of speeches. Westmoreland—every inch the crisp, determined military leader—said:

> I am absolutely certain that whereas in 1965 the enemy was winning, today he is certainly losing. . . . We are making progress. We know you want an honorable and early transition. . . . So do your sons and so do I. It lies within our grasp—the enemy's hopes are bankrupt. With your support we will give you a success.

But Westmoreland secretly asked Johnson to send more troops. Despite the brave words, the war was far from over. Secretary of Defense McNamara knew this too, even though he continued to issue lists of statistics to prove otherwise. In private, he joined the doves and told Johnson that the war could not be won. But Johnson was too deeply committed to the war to admit defeat. He made plans to replace McNamara. By the end of the following year, 1968, the fighting would spread to the streets of America, and both Johnson and Westmoreland would also be swept aside.

At an antiwar rally in Dallas, Texas, a woman has pinned a familiar slogan to the shirt of her two-year-old son. Note the American flag flying upside down—a traditional sign of distress. (AP/Wide World)

CHAPTER TEN

1968—The Year of the Monkey

May you live in interesting times.

—Ancient Chinese curse

SEVERAL hours after dusk on the second day of 1968, a sentry dog's barking alerted marines at Khe Sanh (pronounced Kay Sahn), a remote base in the far northwest of South Vietnam. A squad sent to investigate saw six men in American uniforms walking outside the barbed-wire perimeter. The marines called out a challenge, and the men hesitated—too long. The marines opened fire, killing five of them.

Papers on their bodies showed that the intruders were high-ranking officers in the North Vietnamese Army. What kind of mission could have drawn the North Vietnamese officers so close to such an isolated base?

Back in MACV headquarters in Saigon, General Westmoreland thought he knew the answer. Since mid-December, he had been receiving reports of a big enemy troop build-up around Khe Sanh. Westmoreland had sent spy planes over the area, with electronic devices that could detect cooking fires and even the sweat and urine of men hiding in the dense forests below. The spy planes revealed that thousands of enemy soldiers had encircled Khe Sanh.

On January 20, a North Vietnamese deserter carrying a white flag appeared at Khe Sanh. He revealed that the base would be attacked the following day. The base commander put his men on full alert.

The defector had an even more amazing story. He said the Viet Cong were planning a huge nationwide offensive during the Tet holiday, which would begin only a week later. The news was flashed back to Westmoreland. Thus began 1968, one of the most explosive years in American history.

In the predawn hours of January 21, from six miles away, North Vietnamese artillery opened up on Khe Sanh, and NVA troops stormed the hills around the base. The ground attacks were beaten back, but the artillery scored a direct hit on Khe Sanh's main ammunition dump. Its 1,500 tons of explosives blew sky-high. The shock wave from the blast knocked down tents and buildings. Helicopters parked on the airstrip tumbled onto their sides, and the steel matting on the runway curled up. Men standing hundreds of yards away were smashed to the ground like toy soldiers.

The North Vietnamese had cut the main road to the base, so it had to be resupplied by air with "beans, bullets, and bandages"—military shorthand for food, ammunition, and medical supplies. But the supply aircraft had to land under constant artillery fire. To speed off-loading, rollers were attached to the floor of each cargo plane. As the planes taxied in, they kept their engines running while their cargo was rolled out through a hatch in the rear. Then they continued down the runway and took off again. The only time they stopped was when medics ran forward with wounded men on stretchers to be taken aboard.

After the first large ground attacks, Khe Sanh developed into a siege—as at Dien Bien Phu. Day after day, the base's 6,000 marines holed up in their trenches and bunkers, waiting for the incoming shell that was marked for them. Enemy ground forces crept to within a few hundred yards of the base, and twenty-four hours a day, marines kept their eyes on the concertina-wire perimeter, ready to set off the claymore mines if the enemy attacked.

The base became a prison. Men moved furtively from bunker to bunker, risking a sniper's bullet whenever they went outside. Even running was difficult when the ground shook from the artillery firing back at the enemy. This kind of fighting was particularly hard on marines. They were trained to attack, not defend.

Among Khe Sanh's many horrors were the huge rats that infested the marines' bunkers. Falling asleep without preparations became risky. Marine Johnny Bryant recalled: "You took a blanket and you tucked in like a cocoon. If you didn't, well the first night there a guy showed us what would happen. He refused to sleep with his face covered and a rat bit a hunk out of his face. The rats owned Khe Sanh. We were just roomers."

Far from Khe Sanh, the man who lived in the White House shared the anxiety of the besieged marines. President Johnson knew that the war was losing him support at home—and 1968 was an election year. He had been in Congress during the Battle of Dien Bien Phu. He feared that Khe Sanh would be a replay of the French defeat if the marines could not hold out. ''We don't want one of them 'Din Bin Phoos,' '' Johnson told his aides.

The White House took on the air of a military command post. In the basement, Johnson had a sand-table model of the area around Khe Sanh. As reports came in on the progress of the battle, they were marked on the table. Sometimes, in the middle of the night, the sleepless President would come downstairs in his bathrobe to check what was happening. He went so far as to demand that the Joint Chiefs of Staff give a written guarantee

January 1968. Enemy artillery begins to bombard the marine base at Khe Sanh. Here, one of the shells hits an ammunition dump and blows it sky-high. (Robert Ellison/Black Star)

A U.S. transport plane air-drops supplies to Khe Sanh. The North Vietnamese had cut off the main road to the base. (Courtesy of U.S. Army)

that the marines could hold the base. The marines at Khe Sanh heard of this and felt ashamed. The President was losing his confidence—in them and in himself.

General Westmoreland, on the other hand, felt Khe Sanh "could be the greatest battle" of the war. The war had dragged on for nearly three years. The search-and-destroy missions had not wiped out the Viet Cong, and North Vietnamese reinforcements continued down the Ho Chi Minh

Trail. Like the French commander in 1954, Westmoreland wanted to draw the enemy into a major battle. Khe Sanh, he thought, was that opportunity. It would give him the chance to deal Giap's forces a stunning blow.

Westmoreland knew there were major differences between Khe Sanh and Dien Bien Phu. The Khe Sanh base was on an easily defended plateau, not in a valley. Though the roads to the base had been cut, American supply planes continued to fly into Khe Sanh throughout the battle. Marines held the surrounding hills as well—from fire bases there, artillery guns pounded the North Vietnamese. At Khe Sanh, the outgoing shells outnumbered the incoming by a ratio of twenty to one.

The Americans also had giant B-52 bombers, which dropped more than 100,000 tons of bombs on the Communist troops around Khe Sanh. Khe Sanh became the most heavily bombed area in history. But the North Vietnamese hid their artillery guns in caves—just as they had fourteen years earlier at Dien Bien Phu—rolling them out to shoot and then rolling them back. The B-52s could not silence them.

Even so, Westmoreland's confidence was justified. In April, American forces blasted their way through Route 9, the main road from Da Nang, and the 77-day siege ended. Reinforcements poured into Khe Sanh. But when they spread out into the countryside, they found few North Vietnamese. As always, the enemy had melted away and gone elsewhere to fight again another day. In late June, marines bulldozed the remaining buildings at Khe Sanh and then abandoned it.

Khe Sanh was no longer important because the major battles Westmoreland had wanted had taken place somewhere else. General Giap had attacked Khe Sanh only to distract the Americans and draw their forces to an isolated spot. The Vietnamese defector had been correct—a week after the siege began, the enemy had brought the war into the cities of South Vietnam.

A truce had been called for the celebration of Tet, the Vietnamese New Year, from January 27 to February 3. In Saigon, celebrations were under way to usher in the Year of the Monkey. (In Vietnam, each year in a twelve-year cycle is given a different animal's name.) Many South Vietnamese troops had gone to their home villages to be with their families. Others lolled in the cafés of Saigon, toasting the New Year. Though Westmoreland's staff had received the deserter's warning from Khe Sanh

U.S. soldiers wade through the high elephant grass on their way to the besieged marine base at Khe Sanh. In April, American forces blasted their way through Route 9, the main road to Khe Sanh, and the 77-day siege ended. (AP/Wide World)

January 1968. A mother of three tries to make her way to safety in Saigon amid the death and destruction of the Tet offensive. (National Archives)

that an attack was planned, few took it seriously. Saigon, like the other major cities, seemed secure. Except for an occasional bomb planted on a street corner, the enemy had always stayed out in the villages, where he was strongest.

Throngs of people crowded into the capital to celebrate the holiday. Among them were VC soldiers dressed as civilians. They had stockpiled ammunition and guns in the city, bringing some of it in the coffins of funeral processions. For just as Nguyen Hue had done 180 years before against the Chinese, General Giap had planned a full-scale attack on the Tet holiday.

Around 2:30 A.M. on January 31, a taxi and a small truck drew up outside the U.S. embassy compound in Saigon. Special VC "death-defying volunteers" leaped out. They blasted their way right through the wall around the compound. For six hours, a battle raged between the VC and the embassy's marine guards. American civilians inside the embassy fired pistols and rifles from the windows. They telephoned desperately for help. Finally, troops arrived and wiped out the VC attackers. The embassy building remained secure—at the cost of several marines' lives—but fighting continued all over the city.

Wearing red armbands so that they could identify each other, VC had attacked targets all over Saigon. They captured the government radio station and called for the people to join the fight. "Throw out the Americans," they cried, "and their puppet, President Thieu!"

Westmoreland was awakened at 3 A.M. Hundreds of reports of similar attacks were pouring in from all over the country. Every one of South Vietnam's provinces and more than a hundred towns and cities had been attacked by the Viet Cong. At the White House, where it was late afternoon, the news threw the President's staff into confusion. No one had believed that the enemy was strong enough for such an offensive.

Westmoreland rallied his forces. The first task was to regain control of Saigon. The VC had captured many parts of the city and were attacking Tan Son Nhut airport. If the airport fell, Westmoreland would be unable to fly in reinforcements. By luck, a large South Vietnamese force was waiting there. They had been assigned to fly out the night before, but their planes had been delayed. They fought off the VC and saved the airport.

Soon American tanks were rumbling through the streets of the city, bombarding buildings where the VC were hiding. Casualties were high on all sides. People who had fled from the fighting in the countryside were now caught in the crossfire. To clear the city, U.S. planes finally had to bomb some Viet Cong–held areas.

The head of South Vietnam's national police force executes a Viet Cong prisoner during the Tet offensive. Recorded on film, the brutal scene was replayed on American television, creating more doubts about the conduct of our South Vietnamese allies. (AP/Wide World)

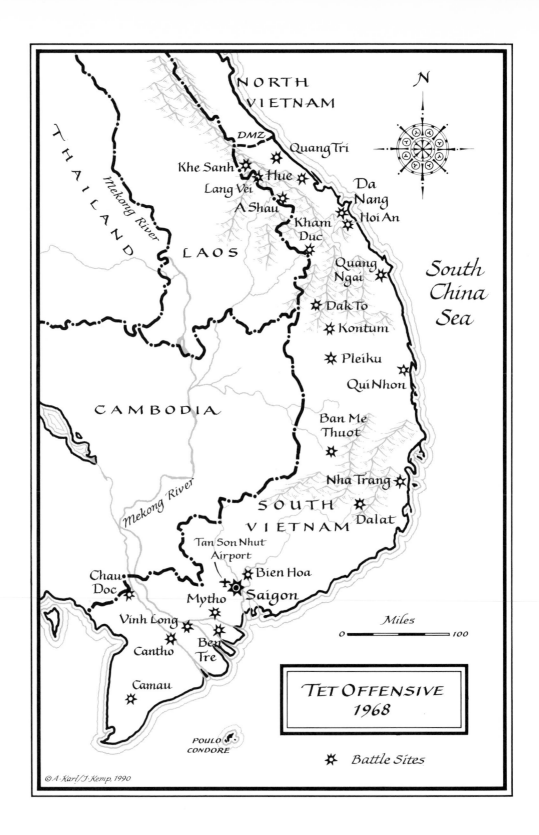

NORTH
VIETNAM

DMZ

Quang Tri

Khe Sanh
Hue
Lang Vei
A Shau
Da
Nang
Hoi An
Kham
Duc
Quang
Ngai
Dak To
Kontum
Pleiku
Qui Nhon

Ban Me
Thuot

Nha Trang
Dalat

THAILAND

Mekong River

LAOS

CAMBODIA

Mekong River

SOUTH
VIETNAM

Tan Son Nhut
Airport
Bien Hoa
Chau
Doc
Saigon
Mytho
Vinh Long
Ben
Tre
Cantho
Camau

POULO
CONDORE

South
China
Sea

N

Miles
0   100

TET OFFENSIVE
1968

✿ Battle Sites

© A. Karl / J. Kemp, 1990

Even then, Saigon was not completely safe. Thousands more Viet Cong had gathered in villages surrounding the city, ready to sweep in. When Westmoreland learned this, he ordered airstrikes against the villages. After the bombing of one such town, Ben Tre (pronounced Ben Tray), an American major said to a reporter, "We had to destroy it to save it." This unwise comment, made in the heat of battle, was widely reported in the United States. To many, it summed up the whole American effort in Vietnam.

In the rest of the country, American airpower and hard fighting on the ground destroyed the VC. Within days, most of the towns it had taken were back under South Vietnamese or American control.

But for nearly a month, the enemy grimly held on to the former imperial city of Hue. North Vietnamese troops had captured the city on the first day of Tet. ARVN troops tried to retake it, but made little progress. American marines went in to help them. Fighting was block to block and sometimes hand to hand. The North Vietnamese were entrenched in homes and shops. Down each street, the marines ran a gauntlet of gunfire. Marine John Moore recalled: "I dove over a wall after crossing the street a couple of times. Cement chips and branches flew everywhere. It was so bad we couldn't even pop up and fire."

As the marines fought their way through Hue, the North Vietnamese retreated into the Citadel, once the palace complex of the Vietnamese emperors. Though the last emperor was now gone forever, the palace stood as a symbol of Vietnam's glorious past. In a strange way, though the fighting was bloody, the marines were glad that they had cornered a foe who could not melt back into the jungles. Now they had a real objective to capture.

Both sides fought ferociously. There were many buildings in the palace complex, and each one had to be cleared room by room. North Vietnamese died at their machine guns, killed by marine grenades or American bombers.

Toward the end of the battle, a marine sergeant moved through the palace. Frightened and sweating, with his M-16 in hand, he went cautiously from room to room until he reached the heart of the palace—the throne room. He stared at the double thrones and gold leaf walls, feeling like a knight who had stormed a castle. As light filtered through the windows, he saw two North Vietnamese lying on the floor. He poked them with his rifle, but they were dead. The Tet offensive was over.

But the cost had been great. By some estimates as much as 75 percent of Hue had been destroyed. Particularly horrifying was the discovery of a

mass grave of 2,800 South Vietnamese civilians. They had been on execution lists carried by the North Vietnamese when they captured the city.

Westmoreland declared proudly that his forces had won a great victory. He had good reason to think so. The Tet offensive had been carried out largely by the Viet Cong. They had gambled their strength and lost. By coming out in the open, they made themselves vulnerable. At least 50,000 of them had been killed, and they were unable to hold on to the towns they had won. The Viet Cong were permanently weakened as a fighting force. From this point on, North Vietnamese troops would fight the war without much help from the Viet Cong.

In addition, the South Vietnamese people had not responded to the VC's call for a major uprising. They remained loyal to the government. But civilians had been hardest hit in the countrywide fighting. American bombers and artillery had flattened many towns. Refugees whose homes had been destroyed roamed the countryside. One out of every twelve South Vietnamese was now homeless.

LEFT: *Two soldiers drag a wounded American to safety during the fighting at Hue.*
BELOW: *Pictures and letters from loved ones lie scattered around this dead North Vietnamese soldier, a reminder of the terrible human cost of the war to Vietnam. (Donald McCullin/Magnum)*

However, the Communists had shown that they could attack anywhere in South Vietnam. Though Westmoreland declared Tet a victory, Americans at home had a very different picture of it.

When people in the United States saw the Tet offensive on television, they were shocked. Johnson and his officials had assured the nation that the war was almost over. Their words came back to haunt them. Now it seemed that even the U.S. embassy, the most visible symbol of American power in Vietnam, was not safe. Americans felt they had been lied to once again.

Walter Cronkite, the anchor for the CBS evening newscast, was one of those whose faith in the war was shaken by Tet. As he stood in the newsroom, reading the Teletype reports of the offensive, he exclaimed, "What the hell is going on? I thought we were winning the war."

Cronkite visited the battlefields of Vietnam in February. He saw firsthand the desperate fighting at Khe Sanh and in other parts of the country. His trip left him pessimistic about the future of the war. In a break with news-show tradition, he stated on his evening program that the war was a stalemate that could not be won. Cronkite's calm, steady manner had won him the respect of many Americans over the years. President Johnson was aware of the powerful effect of television—he had three sets in his office so that he could watch all of the network newscasts. When he heard Cronkite's editorial, he said, "If I've lost Walter, then I've lost Mr. Average Citizen."

That was true. The real victory of the Tet offensive was in the battle for the hearts and minds of the American people. Opinion polls showed a sharp drop in American support for the war. For the first time, a majority of Americans had doubts about a war their country was fighting. Some politicians now openly criticized the war. When Secretary of Defense McNamara said that the Tet offensive had failed, Republican Senator George Aiken of Vermont retorted, "If this is failure, I hope the Viet Cong never have a major success."

The debate over Vietnam had by now split Johnson's Democratic party and even his own advisers. Despite McNamara's brave words about Tet, he too had lost faith in the war. Johnson replaced him with Clark Clifford in February 1968. But Clifford himself soon had doubts. In one of his first acts as secretary of defense, he asked the top military brass for their plans and goals in Vietnam. He was astonished that no one could give him clear answers on how long the war would last or even whether we were winning. The military's only strategy was a vague hope that we would finally wear the enemy down. Now Westmoreland wanted more troops to take advantage of the Tet "victory."

Johnson could not call up more troops to go to Vietnam. It was an election year. Most presidents do not face challengers for reelection from within their own party, but Johnson had two. In March, Senator Eugene McCarthy came close to defeating Johnson in the New Hampshire primary. A few days later, Senator Robert Kennedy, the brother of the assassinated president, declared himself a candidate.

Though most expected Johnson to defend his policies by making a strong bid for reelection, he startled the country in a televised speech on March 31. Calling once again for the North to agree to peace talks, he said that the bombing of the North would stop, except for a small area around the DMZ. Then he ended his speech with a shocker: "I shall not seek, and I will not accept, the nomination of my party for another term as your President." Exhausted by the war and suffering from ill health, the President decided to devote his remaining months in office to trying to achieve peace.

The horrors of 1968 continued. On April 4, civil rights leader Martin Luther King, Jr., was shot on the balcony of a Memphis motel. His death set off riots in many American cities as enraged blacks burned stores and overturned police cars. In Vietnam, black soldiers were stricken with grief and anger. As one of them wrote: "How [could I] be trying to protect foreigners in their country when my hero can't even walk the streets [of America]?"

In the year before he died, King had spoken out against the Vietnam War. He saw it as a waste of young men and American resources in an attempt to destroy a poor Asian nation. But he had always advised his followers to remain nonviolent in the pursuit of their rights. With his death, the nation lost one of its strongest voices for peace at home and abroad.

In May, students at New York City's Columbia University staged a protest against the university's policy of accepting money from the Defense Department for scientific research. The protesters took over the administration building and wrecked the dean's office. Police were called in to drive students from the building. On other campuses, student protests grew increasingly angry and violent.

Two months after King's death, an assassin struck down another American leader. Robert Kennedy won the California presidential primary on June 5. He told a crowd of cheering supporters, "I think we can end the divisions within the United States, the violence." As he left the victory celebration through a hotel kitchen, a gunman stepped from the shadows and fired a .22-caliber bullet into his brain. Kennedy died the following day.

Americans were numbed by Kennedy's assassination, so soon after King's and so hauntingly like the death of Kennedy's brother only five years before. The country seemed to be coming apart, racked by violence and torn by the angry debate over Vietnam.

Against this setting, the Democratic party met in Chicago in August to choose its candidate for president. Inside the convention hall, antiwar candidate Eugene McCarthy was pitted against Johnson's vice-president, Hubert H. Humphrey. Outside, in the streets of Chicago, the war had come home. Some radical groups, such as the Yippies (Youth International Party), had come to Chicago to create chaos and anarchy. Yippie leaders Abbie Hoffman and Jerry Rubin held their own convention in a local park and nominated a pig for president. Afterward, their followers taunted Chicago's police with shouts of "Pig!"

All the negative qualities of the antiwar movement were on display in Chicago. Wild-eyed demonstrators chanted obscene slogans and taunted citizens dressed in suits and ties. Rumors were floated that the Yippies would put the drug LSD in the city's water supply. Left to themselves, the demonstrators would have influenced few Americans. But they had an unwitting ally in Chicago's mayor, Richard Daley.

Daley wanted the convention to be a showcase for his city, and he was determined that no long-haired hippies would spoil it. He had prepared his police force to control 100,000 antiwar demonstrators. Although only 10,000 showed up, they had an effect far beyond their numbers. They taunted police with obscene gestures, rocks, and firecrackers, and the police responded with tear gas and clubs. One injured demonstrator shinnied up a flag pole and replaced the American flag with his bloody shirt. The enraged police waded into the crowd around the pole, calling "Kill, kill, kill!" as they swung their nightsticks. In their wild attacks, the police sometimes clubbed people who were just walking by.

Demonstrators planned their actions for the benefit of television. In the evening, they gathered in front of a large hotel where many delegates were staying. As the police rushed forward to drive them back with fists and nightsticks, floodlights from the TV cameras lit up the scene. The crowd chanted gleefully, "The whole world is watching!" knowing that the police violence was being carried into millions of homes.

The violence, and its effects, seeped into the convention hall. From the speaker's podium, Senator Abraham Ribicoff described the fighting outside the hall. He denounced Mayor Daley, one of the most prominent

August 1968. Antiwar protesters went to Chicago, Illinois, in force for the Democratic National Convention. Here, a group has raised Viet Cong flags over a statue in Grant Park, on the city's lakefront. When some protesters camped out in the park, Chicago police officers drove them off with tear gas and clubs. (AP/Wide World)

members of the Democratic party. TV cameras showed the red-faced Daley shouting back from his seat in the Illinois delegation. Fights broke out among the delegates, and the Chicago police entered the convention hall. By now they regarded all TV reporters as enemies, and NBC correspondent John Chancellor was arrested and dragged off the floor.

Hubert Humphrey won the nomination, but his victory was a hollow one. He had almost no chance of winning, because the delegates went home as they had come—divided between those who supported and those who opposed the war. The convention had shown Americans a party as deeply split as the nation itself.

A month later, the Republican convention presented a sharp contrast. With patriotic speeches, the Republicans nominated Richard Nixon, who had based his political career on anticommunism. He had firmly supported U.S. involvement in Vietnam from his days as Eisenhower's vice-president. However, he realized that the war was unpopular. He gave Americans hope that he would find a way out of Vietnam. He said he had a secret plan to end the war. This boosted his popularity in the opinion polls.

Humphrey's only hope was that the government could negotiate a truce before the election. Peace talks had begun in Paris in May—but for months the main topics of discussion had been who should attend and what the shape of the table should be.

At first, North Vietnam wanted to talk only with the United States, refusing to meet South Vietnam's representatives. After both South Vietnam and the NLF (National Liberation Front) were included, the United States insisted that because there were only two sides in the war, they should sit opposite each other. But the North wanted a four-sided table—representing the United States, South Vietnam, the NLF, and North Vietnam. Though the argument seemed stupid, it reflected the bitter divisions between the two sides. While the squabble over the table went on, people continued to die in Vietnam.

At the end of October, Johnson announced a complete bombing halt above the 17th parallel. Operation Rolling Thunder was over, after three years, eight months, and twenty-four days. American bombers had flown 100,000 missions and dropped half a million tons of bombs. But they had not won the war.

The bombing halt was too late for the Democrats. The fighting did not stop, and Nixon won the election on November 6. The nation looked to him to solve the problem of Vietnam.

CHAPTER ELEVEN

The End of the Tunnel

We have finally achieved peace with honor.

—Richard Nixon, 1973

ON January 20, 1969, Richard Nixon was sworn in as President. Nixon was very different from Johnson, in both his interests and his personality. While Johnson concentrated on domestic problems, Nixon had long studied global affairs, preparing himself to be "the leader of the free world." Johnson had enjoyed the give-and-take of politics, the handshaking, arm-twisting, and personal contact with others. Nixon, on the other hand, was a loner and secretive by nature.

During the campaign, Nixon had read an article on Vietnam by Henry Kissinger, a professor of government at Harvard University. Kissinger had written that Vietnam was a test of America's credibility—the United States, having given its word to defend South Vietnam, must now do so. Impressed by Kissinger's views, Nixon chose him as his main foreign policy adviser. Kissinger shared Nixon's secretive traits. He would work closely with Nixon in the White House and serve as his personal ambassador on secret missions.

Nixon knew that the American people wanted to end the fighting—but not by running away from Vietnam. He intended to win "peace with honor" at the negotiating table. He believed he could achieve his goal by frightening the North Vietnamese. Nixon explained to an aide:

> I call it the Madman theory. . . . I want the North Vietnamese to believe that I've reached the point where I might do anything to stop the war. We'll just slip the word to them that, "For God's sake, you know Nixon is obsessed about Communists. We can't restrain him when he's angry—and he has his hand on the nuclear button"—and Ho Chi Minh himself will be in Paris in two days begging for peace.

It would not be that easy.

January 1969. An American prisoner of war being guarded by a North Vietnamese soldier. Many prisoners were held in an old French fort in Hanoi which Americans mockingly called the Hanoi Hilton. (Courtesy of U.S. Army)

Nixon didn't really have a secret plan for defeating the North—that was campaign rhetoric. What he wanted to do was to shift the burden of the fighting onto the South Vietnamese. This policy was called Vietnamization. It was a long word that meant, in effect, what President Johnson had called for when he said American boys should not do the fighting for Asian boys.

Nixon did not intend to simply abandon the South. The American withdrawal would be a gradual one. American airpower would continue to provide support. But by cutting down on American casualties, Nixon would gain time to negotiate a settlement. On June 8, he met with President Thieu on Midway, an island in the Pacific Ocean. Thieu publicly approved a greater role for the South Vietnamese army. "We have claimed for years that we were getting stronger," he said. "If it is so, we have to be willing to see some Americans leave."

At the conference, Nixon announced the withdrawal of 25,000 American troops. The American public breathed a sigh of relief.

American hopes rose in September when Ho Chi Minh died. Although Nixon made no public comment, a Washington official described the emotions in the White House as "something close to elation." Nixon hoped that with Ho gone, the North Vietnamese would be more willing to negotiate.

In North Vietnam, the people were stunned by Ho's death. His body lay in state in the public square in Hanoi, where, twenty-four years earlier, he had proclaimed the independence of Vietnam. Tens of thousands of mourners passed by his funeral bier.

But his death did nothing to soften the North's goal of unifying the country. Giap, Dong, and the other North Vietnamese leaders knew that American troop withdrawal would give them a chance to win. The "end of the tunnel" appeared closer.

Nixon had set no timetable for pulling out. But he knew that once the process began, Americans would be impatient for all of their sons and husbands to come home. The difficult task of Vietnamization was turned over to General Creighton Abrams, the new head of MACV. (Westmoreland had returned home to become Chief of Staff of the Army.) Abrams began a crash program to train South Vietnamese troops and officers. The United States started to turn over its vast arsenal of weapons and equipment to the South.

Much of this equipment had to be operated by skilled people. Many American soldiers had grown up tinkering with automobile engines. They could apply this experience to planes, helicopters, tanks, and armored personnel carriers. But most Vietnamese had grown up in villages where farmers used buffaloes instead of tractors. There were no helicopter maintenance manuals written in Vietnamese—the language did not even have the technological words to deal with such things. Pilots and mechanics had to be taught English before their training could begin. Progress was agonizingly slow, and time was short.

At Nixon's urging, Thieu took some of the steps that should have been taken long before. He allowed his people to elect their own village officials and province chiefs. Villagers were given a greater say in deciding

President Nixon wanted to shift the burden of fighting onto the South Vietnamese. Here, South Vietnamese soldiers attack a bullet-scarred building where North Vietnamese soldiers are hiding. (The Bettmann Archive)

how American aid was to be used. Thieu took land owned by absentee landlords and distributed it to the peasants. He offered amnesty—a full pardon—and a cash payment to any Viet Cong who surrendered. Because of the military failure of the Tet offensive, many Viet Cong accepted the offer.

Americans continued to fight in combat. In May 1969, a large group of North Vietnamese was spotted on a hill in the A Shau Valley (pronounced Ah Show) in the northwest part of South Vietnam. The American commanders ordered an attack. On military maps, the hill was named Hill 937. But because it chewed up so many American soldiers, it was dubbed Hamburger Hill.

The North Vietnamese were tightly bunkered in at the top of the hill. They beat back the first assault. American artillery and air strikes stripped the hill bare of all vegetation. Heavy rains turned it into a mudslide. Each time the Americans tried to move up, they were mowed down by enemy fire. It took eleven assaults to capture the hill. Forty-six Americans were killed and three hundred were wounded.

Just a month after the hill was finally taken, it was abandoned. The troops were bitter. Hamburger Hill seemed to stand for the futility of the Vietnam War. Near the landing zone, some troops put up a cardboard sign: "Hamburger Hill. Was it worth it?"

American troops now knew they weren't going to win the war. Sooner or later they would be ordered home. All of them were now short-timers—with only weeks or months left to serve. No one knew exactly when his unit would be called in, but they all knew that they were fighting a lost cause.

No one wanted to be the last soldier to die in Vietnam. Soldiers often refused orders to go on patrol in hostile areas. In some units, men killed officers who they believed unnecessarily endangered their lives. This was called fragging, because fragmentation grenades were often the weapon of choice. An underground troop newspaper carried a reward of $10,000 for the man who fragged the commander who had ordered the attacks at Hamburger Hill. (The reward was never collected.)

During the 1960s, many young Americans tried marijuana, and its use was common among soldiers. But in Vietnam, more powerful drugs were widely available. Laos was (and still is) one of the world's major sources of opium, which can be turned into heroin. High-quality heroin was cheap and easy to buy. Many soldiers turned to it to ease their pain and anxiety.

The soldiers' morale also suffered from the continuing racial conflict in the United States. At home, the slogan "Black Power" stood for black people's determination to win equal treatment, by force if necessary. In Vietnam, black soldiers decided not to put up with such things as Confederate flags displayed by Southern white soldiers, and fights broke out in base areas between black and white soldiers.

But in combat, racial problems usually faded before the common goal of staying alive. What kept the men together was a sense of pride and loyalty to each other. William Broyles, an officer in Vietnam, wrote later:

> There grew up in Vietnam combat units a sense of commitment and love among the men who lived, laughed, suffered and died together. You took your turn on point, pushing into the terrible unknown of the jungle or down an exposed rice-paddy dike, you went up a hill under fire, you crawled out after the wounded—not for your country; you did it for your buddies.

Back in the United States, a new revelation further shattered American spirits. More than a year earlier, on March 16, 1968, a terrible event had taken place in a Vietnamese village named My Lai (pronounced Me Lie).

At 7 A.M., helicopters dropped about two hundred American soldiers into the area around My Lai. Before leaving their base, the soldiers had been told by other officers that My Lai was a Viet Cong stronghold. They were to wipe out everyone they found, because, as one soldier recalled later, "those people that were in the village—the women, the kids, the old men—were VC."

The soldiers needed no urging. Not long before, a popular sergeant in the unit had been killed by a Viet Cong booby trap. The men wanted revenge, and when they moved into the village, they showed no mercy.

They began by setting fire to the village huts and raping some of the women and girls. Before long, the men lost all control and started to fire wildly at anything that moved, even the cattle, pigs, and chickens. A large group of villagers were herded into a ditch and raked by machine guns. When one soldier refused to fire, his commanding officer, Lieutenant William Calley, threatened to report him for disobeying an officer's order.

The official report of the action described My Lai as a military victory, with 128 Viet Cong added to the body count. The task-force commander called the mission "well planned, well executed, and successful." Many higher officers knew the real story, but ignored it.

Some of the soldiers who were at My Lai were disturbed by what happened and told others about it. One soldier, who was appalled by what he heard, sent letters to the army and Congress asking for an investigation. But nothing happened until November 1969, when reporter Seymour Hersh broke the story. Dozens of American newspapers printed Hersh's article.

Life magazine obtained photographs of the slaughter from a soldier who had been on the scene. The piled-up bodies of the villagers appeared in full color in one of the country's leading magazines. The American public was stunned. My Lai caused a national soul-searching on the whole question of what we were doing in Vietnam—and what Vietnam was doing to us. The mother of one of the soldiers at My Lai said, "I sent them a good boy, and they made him a murderer."

Three officers and a sergeant who led the troops at My Lai were accused of atrocities, or crimes against civilians. But only Lieutenant William Calley was convicted—in his case, of killing twenty-two people, including babies. Calley's testimony that the My Lai operation was "no big deal" added to Americans' horror and disgust. However, because Calley's superior officers were not punished, many people felt he was a scapegoat who took the blame for a complete breakdown in army discipline.

A military court sentenced Calley to life imprisonment, but the secretary of the army reduced that to ten years. Calley was paroled after serving three years under house arrest at a military base.

Throughout the war, Communist forces had been able to retreat to safety in the neighboring countries of Cambodia and Laos, and President Johnson had not allowed U.S. troops to pursue them. Under President Nixon, this policy changed.

Norodom Sihanouk, Cambodia's leader, had tried to protect his weak country from the war. He believed that North Vietnam would eventually win. For that reason, he allowed the Communists to build sanctuaries in the border areas of Cambodia—bases where they kept supplies and could retreat after battles.

In March 1969, Nixon ordered American planes to bomb the Cambodian sanctuaries. Nixon tried to keep the bombing a secret because he wanted to avoid further protests at home. Even members of Congress were kept in the dark.

But the bombing did not wipe out the sanctuaries. Instead, it only pushed the Communists farther west into the interior of Cambodia. Nixon and his generals decided that it was necessary to invade Cambodia to destroy the sanctuaries once and for all.

A year later, while Sihanouk was on an overseas trip, one of his officials, Lon Nol, took power. He promised to drive the Vietnamese out of the country and ally Cambodia with the United States. The U.S. government was pleased. It now had a green light for action in Cambodia.

On April 30, 1970, ten days after announcing the withdrawal of another 125,000 troops from Vietnam, President Nixon spoke to the American people. He told them that the United States and South Vietnam were invading Cambodia. (He called it an incursion, avoiding the stronger word ''invasion.'') Nixon claimed that the purpose of the incursion was

May 1, 1970. A soldier involved in the invasion of Cambodia reads about the reaction to it on college campuses back home in Stars and Stripes, *the official army newspaper. (Courtesy of U.S. Army)*

not to widen the war, but to protect the American troops that remained in Vietnam.

The invasion met little resistance. Many of the Communist troops, warned of the attack, had already fled westward. But the allied forces captured huge stores of arms and equipment. American troop morale rose, and the operation, which ended on June 30, was hailed as a success.

In the United States, the incursion outraged the public. Antiwar demonstrations broke out on college campuses. At Kent State University in Ohio, someone set fire to the building where students trained to become army officers. Ohio's governor sent National Guard soldiers to the campus. On May 4, a crowd of students leaving classes for lunch began to taunt the troops. The soldiers assumed a combat stance. Suddenly they opened

May 4, 1970. Four students were killed and nine wounded at Kent State University when Ohio National Guard soldiers opened fire on students protesting the Cambodian invasion. News of the killings traveled quickly to campuses all over the country, and hundreds of other universities and colleges closed in protest and sympathy. (Valley Daily News, Tarentum, Pa., John Filo © 1970)

fire, killing four students and wounding nine. Some of these students were hundreds of yards away, and not even aware of the protest.

At Jackson State College in Mississippi, police fired on a student dormitory after another antiwar protest. Two students were killed in their rooms.

Many other colleges closed for the rest of the school year to avoid further violence. The killings at Kent State and Jackson State were yet another sign of how the war had torn the United States apart.

Students weren't the only ones alarmed by the Cambodian invasion. Congress passed a resolution forbidding the further use of American ground troops in Cambodia, and Laos as well. Later that year it repealed the Gulf of Tonkin Resolution, which had given the President the power to wage war without a declaration. But Congress knew that a majority of Americans still did not want to simply surrender and get out. It continued to vote money to carry on the war.

Nixon had been encouraged by the Cambodian invasion. He wanted to strangle the Communists' supply line—the Ho Chi Minh Trail—by invading Laos. But because Congress had forbidden the use of U.S. troops, South Vietnamese forces would have to do the fighting. American bombers, helicopters, and artillery would support the South Vietnamese. It was the first major test of Vietnamization.

In February 1971, ARVN troops advanced slowly into Laos. All went well until they met North Vietnamese resistance. Seeing that they were outnumbered, the ARVN commanders called for American helicopters to get them out.

Photographs told the story of an army withdrawing in panic, with soldiers clinging to the skids of the helicopters. The South Vietnamese casualties were high—as were those for American helicopter pilots and crews: 66 Americans killed, 83 wounded, and 28 listed as missing.

Nixon claimed the operation was a success. Yet anyone who saw the TV and newspaper pictures knew this was not true. The credibility gap between Americans and their government continued to grow.

A surprising leak of secret documents told Americans just how much they had been lied to. Back in 1967, Defense Secretary Robert McNamara had asked his staff to prepare a full record of the decisions that had led to the war. Stamped top secret, the report lay hidden in government files until one of the men who had written it gave a copy to *The New York*

THE MARCH AGAINST DEATH

The largest protest against the war took place in the nation's capital on a bitterly cold November weekend in 1969. It began on the evening of the thirteenth, when 40,000 people gathered near the gates of Arlington National Cemetery, where the nation buries its war heroes. Around their necks, the marchers wore cards with the names of Americans who had been killed in Vietnam. Carrying candles, they crossed Memorial Bridge into the city of Washington and walked around the Lincoln Memorial and up the Mall toward the White House. As each marcher reached the White House, he or she called out the name on the card.

The first person in the line was Judy Droz, from Columbia, Missouri. She carried the name of her husband, who had been killed in April. She said she came to "express my feelings and those of my late husband that the United States should get out of Vietnam immediately. There is no light at the end of the tunnel, only the darkness that came over my husband." The marchers deposited their cards in coffins by the Capitol. All night long the chain of candles could be seen winding through the streets.

Saturday dawned, a cold but sunny day. That morning buses poured into Washington, carrying hundreds of thousands of people from all over the United States. Many had ridden all night long to make their feelings known in a public way.

They gathered at the Capitol building and at 10:30 A.M. began to march down Pennsylvania Avenue. The crowd linked arms in rows seventeen people wide, chanting, "What do we want? Peace! When do we want it? Now!" Wave after wave of them appeared in a seemingly endless line—many young people in bell-bottom jeans and sweatshirts, and thousands of older Americans as well, had come to join the effort to end the war. Three and a half hours later, the last of the marchers reached their destination—the grassy Mall around the Washington Monument.

The crowd was enormous. Though estimates of the actual number varied from 200,000 to 800,000, Washington, D.C., police officials agreed that it was the largest demonstration ever to take place in the capital. Despite the chilly weather, those who stood on the Mall shared a feeling of warmth and good fellowship. Seeing how many others had come to exercise their right to demonstrate, they knew they were part of an historic occasion.

Many demonstrators held banners with such slogans as "End the War Now"; others carried posters showing the faces of Robert Kennedy, Martin Luther King, Jr., and Ho Chi Minh. Still others displayed the peace symbol—an upside-down Y in a circle. A few people waved the Viet Cong flag; many more, the American flag.

Speakers such as antiwar Senator George McGovern and Coretta Scott King, the widow of Martin Luther King, Jr., tried to address the crowd, but they could hardly be heard. Folksinger Pete Seeger rose and began a chant that was taken up by hundreds of thousands of people: "All we are saying . . . is give peace a chance." Thousands held their hands high in the V sign that had come to mean peace. At the end of the day they boarded the buses for the long ride home, elated by the thought that they had done something to end the war and stop the killing.

Times. On June 13, 1971, the *Times* started publishing the so-called Pentagon Papers.

Even though the papers contained nothing from the Nixon administration, Nixon was outraged. He obtained a court order stopping their publication. To many Americans, it seemed as though the President was directly attacking the right of a free press. But in a few days, the Supreme Court ruled against Nixon, and publication of the papers resumed. Soon other newspapers began to print excerpts, and Americans learned that while Johnson's advisers were making rosy predictions about Vietnam in public, they secretly agreed that the war would be long and difficult. By trying to keep the papers under wraps, Nixon only made people worry that the government was still lying about Vietnam—as indeed it was.

While the fighting continued in Vietnam, the peace talks in Paris had gone nowhere. In February 1970, Nixon had sent Henry Kissinger to meet in secret with Le Duc Tho (pronounced Lay Duck Toe), a member of the North Vietnamese government. Tho was a tough opponent for Kissinger—often smiling, rarely saying no but more rarely saying yes.

Nixon and Kissinger moved to put pressure on North Vietnam by isolating it from its two major supporters—the Soviet Union and the People's Republic of China. The Communist bloc that had seemed such a threat to the United States in the 1950s had broken up. The Soviet Union and China were now bitter enemies, and the time seemed ripe for the United States to drive a further wedge between them. To do this, however, it had to reverse its longtime policy of refusing to recognize Red China's government.

Kissinger secretly went to China in 1971 to set up a visit by Nixon the next year. In February 1972 the President made his historic trip to China and met with its aging leader, Mao Zedong. The Chinese promised that they would use their influence to encourage the North Vietnamese to follow "moderate" behavior.

Before Nixon could follow up his China trip with one to the Soviet Union, the North Vietnamese acted. While they had been talking in Paris, they had built up their forces for a new offensive. American troop levels were down to around 95,000, and the North wanted to take as much territory as possible before a cease-fire.

On March 31, 1972, North Vietnam staged a major attack. NVA troops crashed across the DMZ, rolling over the green South Vietnamese troops that had taken the place of American marines. Within a month, the North's forces had taken the city of Quang Tri (pronounced Kwan Tree), the capital of South Vietnam's northern province. South Vietnamese soldiers and civilians fled south along the main coastal road. North Vietnamese troops drove into the Central Highlands. Closer to Saigon, NVA and Viet Cong troops attacked the province capital of An Loc (pronounced Ahn Lock).

Nixon was furious. He sent American planes to support the South Vietnamese army and to hit Hanoi and other targets in North Vietnam. He also ordered the mining of Haiphong harbor, North Vietnam's main supply port. The United States had always avoided doing this because Soviet ships used the harbor, and the Americans did not want to kill Soviet sailors. Nixon gambled that the Soviets would not react by canceling Nixon's upcoming trip to Moscow.

South Vietnam, June 1972. Terrified children, followed by South Vietnamese soldiers, flee from a napalm strike accidentally made by South Vietnamese planes. The girl at center has ripped off her burning clothing. Photos like this one turned thousands of Americans against the war. (AP/Wide World)

The gamble worked. The Soviets welcomed Nixon to Moscow and agreed to use their influence to persuade the North to come to peace terms. Nixon now felt that his hand was strengthened. Neither of North Vietnam's major Communist allies was willing to come to its defense.

With American air support, the South Vietnamese began to gain back some of the territory lost early in the offensive. By mid-July it was clear that the North Vietnamese attack could not succeed. The peace talks in Paris resumed in July, and Nixon claimed a victory for Vietnamization.

In private, though, he was less optimistic. He feared what would happen when U.S. troops were gone. The Saigon government was "the weak link in our whole chain," he wrote in his diary. "The real problem is that the enemy is willing to sacrifice in order to win, while the South Vietnamese simply aren't willing to pay that much of a price in order to avoid losing."

After tough negotiations, Kissinger and Le Duc Tho hammered out an agreement in October 1972. It called for a cease-fire with the soldiers of both sides remaining where they were. This meant that 150,000 North Vietnamese troops could remain in South Vietnam. The agreement called the 17th parallel a truce line—as it had been in the Geneva Accords of 1954. The United States no longer insisted that it was a boundary between two countries—the whole basis for the Vietnam War. The United States had originally said it was defending one nation (South Vietnam) against the invasion of a second nation (North Vietnam). Now the United States was admitting that Vietnam was *one* nation. Sometime in the future, elections would be held in the South. These would include candidates from the Provisional Revolutionary Government (PRG), which governed areas that the Viet Cong controlled in the South.

However, South Vietnam's President Thieu refused to sign the agreement because it allowed North Vietnamese troops to remain in South Vietnam. Nixon was frustrated, because he was in the midst of his own campaign for reelection. His opponent, Senator George McGovern, called for American withdrawal from the war. To reassure Americans, Kissinger appeared at a press conference and declared, "Peace is at hand." Americans voted for Nixon.

After his reelection, Nixon decided on a show of strength. He ordered the heaviest and most controversial bombing of the war. On December 18, 1972, waves of giant B-52 bombers struck Hanoi and Haiphong, hitting factories, neighborhoods, and the city's largest hospital. Hanoi claimed that 2,000 people were killed in the so-called "Christmas bombing." More than 90 American airmen lost their lives when they were shot down by the North's antiaircraft guns.

In January a new agreement was reached in the peace talks. It was not very different from the October one. Nixon had sweetened the deal, making private promises to both Thieu and the North Vietnamese. He told Thieu that if North Vietnam violated the agreement, the United States would "react vigorously." To Hanoi, Nixon pledged billions of dollars to help rebuild North Vietnam. Neither promise was kept.

The Paris Peace Accords were signed on January 27, 1973. "We have

The joy of reunion shines in the faces of this family as they rush toward a freed prisoner of war at Travis Air Force Base in California. (AP/Wide World)

finally achieved peace with honor," President Nixon proudly proclaimed. Just five days earlier, former President Lyndon Johnson had died. He had spent his last years on his ranch in Texas, telling his life story to a biographer. He had wanted to be America's greatest President, but he knew that he would be remembered forever for the Vietnam War.

The peace accords guaranteed the return of all prisoners of war. In February and March, Americans welcomed them back. One of the first Americans to be released was the first to be captured, Lieutenant Everett Alvarez. After arriving at an American air force base in the Philippines, Alvarez spoke to millions of TV viewers: "God bless the President and God bless you, Mr. and Mrs. America," he said. "You did not forget us."

The return of the prisoners brought joy and relief to America. This country's longest and most divisive war was over at last. But for Vietnam, the war had not ended.

three

The End of the Thirty Years' War

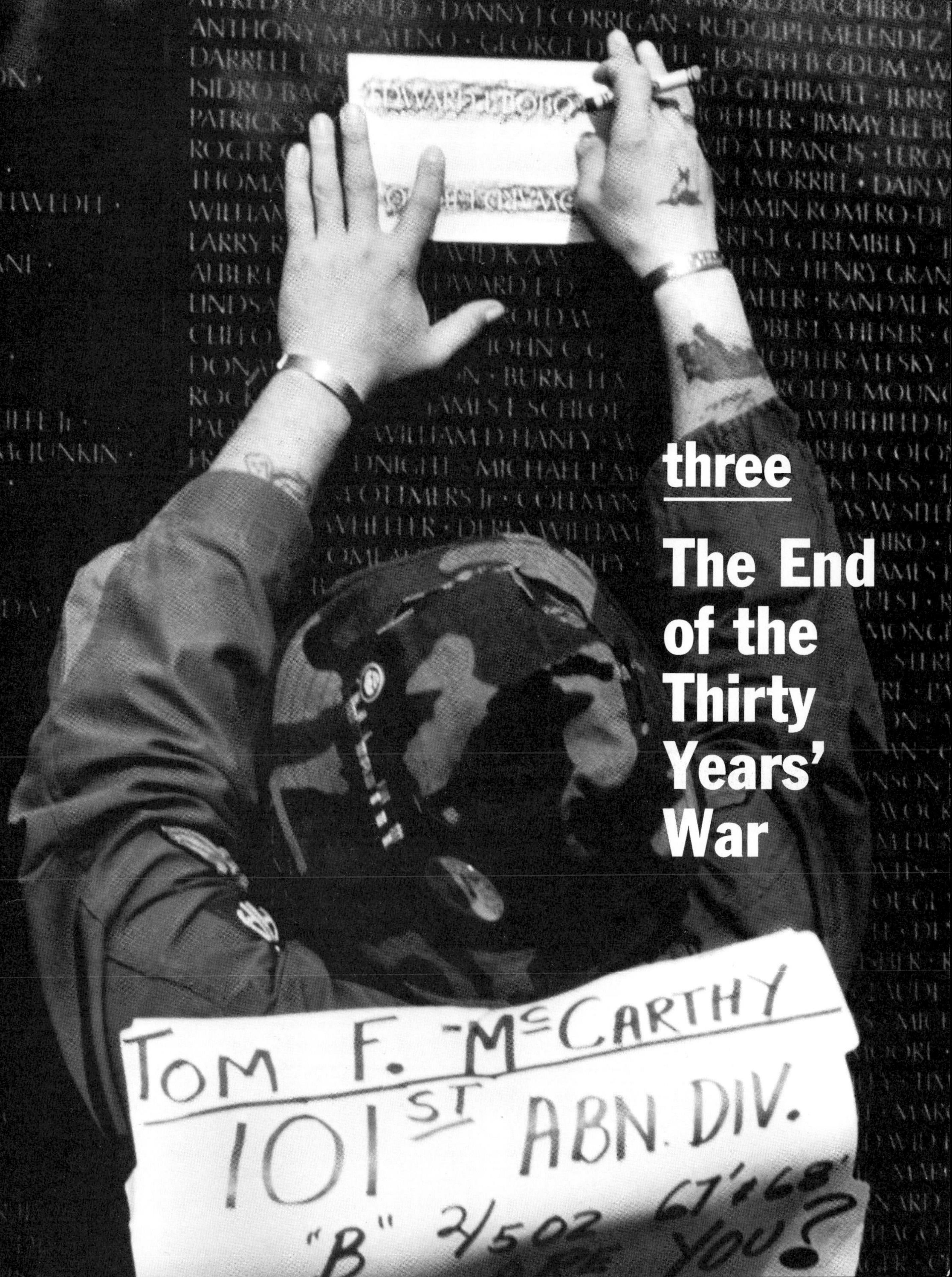

NORTH
VIETNAM

DMZ
Quang Tri
Hue

Da
Nang

Chu
Lai

South
China
Sea

LAOS

THAILAND

Mekong River

Kontum

Pleiku

CAMBODIA

Ban Me Thuot

PHUOC LONG
PROVINCE

SOUTH
VIETNAM

Nha Trang

Cam
Ranh
Bay

Mekong River

An
Loc

Xuan Loc

Miles

0   75

Saigon

Tan
Son Nhut
Airport

Communist Advances

March 1975

April–May 1975

FINAL OFFENSIVE

POULO
CONDORE

N

© A. Karl/J. Kemp, 1990

CHAPTER TWELVE

The Last Helicopter Out

I looked back one last time. . . . After twenty-plus years of war, a city was falling, a government toppling, a country changing. . . . I remember a bit of the briny collecting in the corner of my eye, and my flushed reaction to this unwarriorlike emotionalism. In retrospect, though, when you say a last good-bye to a battleground that took [so many of your] countrymen, I guess it deserves one final tear.

—U.S. fighter pilot who escorted the last American helicopters out of Saigon, April 30, 1975

"THE war is over," Nixon declared in January 1973. Now that the burden of Vietnam was lifted from America's shoulders, Nixon's popularity was at its highest point. Opinion polls showed that he had the support of 70 percent of Americans. The previous November, he had won a huge election victory. But he would never complete his second term. A scandal was about to destroy his presidency.

Nixon's downfall began during his reelection campaign in 1972. On the night of June 16–17, several men were caught breaking into the headquarters of the Democratic party in the Watergate Hotel in Washington, D.C. The men refused to say what they were doing at the hotel, and the Watergate affair remained a "third-rate burglary" until after the election.

In January 1973, however, the case began to crack open. One of the burglars confessed that the men had been hired by Nixon's reelection committee. Someone had paid money to one of the burglars' wives to ensure that no one would talk.

Congress began to investigate. One of Nixon's aides charged that the President had helped to cover up the crime. If so, the evidence would be on the tapes that Nixon used to record conversations in his office. But the President refused to hand over the tapes. "I am not a crook," Nixon told an audience of newspaper editors.

In the fall of 1973, Vice-President Spiro Agnew was accused of accepting bribes and forced to resign. Nixon, with Congress's approval, named Gerald R. Ford, the Republican leader of the House of Representatives, as vice-president.

All during 1974, the country held its breath as the various scandals known as Watergate began to unravel. During the summer the Supreme Court ordered Nixon to turn over his tapes. When they were made public, even his strongest defenders agreed that they showed Nixon was involved in the cover-up. Rather than face impeachment, Nixon resigned on August 8, 1974. Gerald Ford became the first appointed President in U.S. history.

To a nation already demoralized by war and protest, Watergate was a shattering blow. The credibility gap had reduced American faith in the

July 1974. During the Watergate investigation two demonstrators, one wearing a Nixon mask (left) and one wearing a mask of Henry Kissinger, are escorted by police from the front of the Supreme Court building in Washington, D.C. (AP/Wide World)

truthfulness of public officials. Now, Nixon's crimes, and the pardon he was given by President Ford, further shook America's confidence in its leaders.

In Vietnam, it soon became clear that both sides were violating the truce. Both the North and the South moved to increase the territory they controlled within South Vietnam. The North followed a policy of "half war, half peace"—they fought battles to take territory, then built roads and port facilities in these areas.

The Americans encouraged Thieu to increase his base of support. But he did the opposite, becoming more like a dictator. He shut down newspapers and arrested anyone who disagreed with his policies. He stopped allowing the villagers to elect their leaders. These measures only turned the people against him. In late 1973, crowds turned out for a march in memory of President Diem, who had been killed ten years earlier. Even the once-hated Diem, the marchers seemed to be saying, was preferable to their present ruler.

Thieu also faced economic problems. As the Americans left the country, many Vietnamese who had worked for them lost their jobs. Free-spending American soldiers no longer spent their paychecks in South Vietnam's shops. In addition, food prices skyrocketed, and people went hungry. Low-level government officials could earn a living only by taking bribes. Those appointed to lead the villagers stole American aid money meant to help them.

To escape the fighting, refugees flooded into the cities, where there was no room for them. They lived in desperate conditions in shantytowns made of discarded American packing crates and tin cans.

The whole society was coming unglued. South Vietnam, never fully united behind the government, was sinking deeper into corruption and greed. The people's faith in their government dropped to an all-time low.

Many South Vietnamese soldiers deserted. Young men went to any lengths to avoid being drafted into the army. There seemed to be no point in offering one's life for a government that few supported.

Thieu clung to the hope that the Americans would once more come to the rescue. He kept faith in Nixon's promise of American support if there were massive violations of the peace agreements. Thieu did not understand the important changes that had occurred in the United States.

Nixon's promise did not have any legal authority, and Watergate had weakened Nixon even before he resigned. In late 1973, over Nixon's veto, Congress had passed the War Powers Act. This limited the ability of the President to use military power without Congress's approval. And Congress was not about to approve any new American efforts in Vietnam.

The North Vietnamese were much encouraged by Nixon's departure from office in 1974. They had not abandoned their goal of unifying the country. They had enlarged the Ho Chi Minh Trail. Long before, it had grown from its beginnings as a jungle path for human porters. Much of it was now a paved highway, and convoys of trucks streamed down it to supply the Communist forces.

And the North no longer depended on hit-and-run guerrilla tactics. It now fielded a modern army of seasoned troops. In October 1974, the North's military leaders began to plan major offensives for 1975. They were aiming at total victory in 1976. For once, they were too pessimistic.

At the end of 1974, North Vietnamese troops swept into Phuoc Long province, close to Saigon. Within three weeks they had captured its capital city. The attack was intended to test the Americans' reaction. The North Vietnamese feared a renewal of the bombing that had ravaged their country. But there was no reaction from the United States—not even a threat. Politically, there was no way that President Ford could send back troops or support the South with American airpower. For the United States, Vietnam had once more become an unimportant country in a distant part of the world.

In February 1975, preparing for the next stage of the assault, General Van Tien Dung secretly went south to take command of the North Vietnamese forces. Dung had been Giap's chief of staff during the Battle of Dien Bien Phu and was now the North's chief military officer. Joining him on the trip south was Le Duc Tho—who had negotiated the "peace" with Kissinger. To conceal General Dung's departure, a look-alike stayed in his office. In the South, Dung and Tho wore peasant clothing and rode bicycles.

The first target of the 1975 campaign was the town of Ban Me Thuout (pronounced Bahn May Twoat) in the Central Highlands. The North's plan was the same as it had been ten years earlier, when the first American combat troops were sent to Vietnam: The NVA troops would march east to the sea, splitting South Vietnam in half. Ban Me Thuout was taken on March 11 after a one-day fight.

Thieu appealed to the United States for support. When he realized that it was not coming, he made a fateful decision. He and his generals decided to abandon the Central Highlands and move their troops to the coastal cities. But the South's soldiers panicked as they withdrew, and what began as a retreat turned into a rout. Civilians fled along with the soldiers in what came to be called "the convoy of tears." Communist artillery fired on them as they fled. One Vietnamese journalist wrote:

> Many trucks were crammed with soldiers, children, old people. They fell everywhere. Those who walked fell to the machine-gun bullets. Their blood flowed in tiny streams. The roaring artillery, crackling small arms, screams of the dying and crying of children combined into a single voice from hell.

By March 21, Dung's forces had leapfrogged north, surrounding the coastal city of Hue. The United States sent ships to the South China Sea to help evacuate the soldiers. The South Vietnamese commander fled, abandoning his troops. They rushed toward the beach, threw away their rifles, and swam out to the ships. Dung continued his offensive, and the North Vietnamese began to move south along the coast, plucking the cities one by one.

By this time, the South Vietnamese army was in full retreat. Those who tried to regroup and make a stand were hampered by the thousands of civilians who were fleeing with them. They clogged the main roads, making it impossible for trucks or troop transports to get through. Most soldiers followed the lead of their commanders and simply fled. As they ran, they stripped off their uniforms, hoping to receive lenient treatment as civilians.

Dung approached South Vietnam's second largest city, Da Nang. Refugees had swollen the population to one and a half million people—three times its former size. Food was scarce, and panic swept through the city. Everyone was trying to get out before the North Vietnamese arrived. On a refugee ship in the harbor, South Vietnamese marines shot at people to drive them off the overflowing decks.

An American airline flew a jumbo jet into Da Nang to rescue some of the people. Crowds gathered at the airport and charged the plane. Vietnamese soldiers shoved women and children aside in the race to board the plane. As the plane took off, some clung desperately to its landing gear, only to fall to their deaths. As one reporter wrote, "Only the fastest, the strongest, and the meanest of a huge mob got a ride on the last plane from Da Nang Saturday."

When Da Nang fell on March 30, more than 100,000 leaderless South Vietnamese troops surrendered. Americans watched the dreadful scenes on their television screens. It was like losing the war a second time. Men who had fought to defend such places as Pleiku and Da Nang saw them abandoned and knew that their sacrifice had been in vain. Those who had lost a son or a husband were enraged by the cowardice of the South Vietnamese troops. These were our allies in the fight for freedom.

As the South Vietnamese army collapsed, it left behind billions of dollars in American military equipment. The North's soldiers picked up as many weapons as they could carry. Artillery, planes, helicopters—and the gigantic military bases—were theirs for the taking. After the war, Vietnam became one of the world's strongest military powers—courtesy of the United States government.

The North's leaders had thought they would need two years to conquer the South. By the end of March, they realized that Saigon would be theirs in a month. Their soldiers met almost no resistance. A schoolteacher recalled their attitude when they came to her village: "They were so confident when they caught us they just let us go. They laughed at us for running. They said, 'Wherever you run, we will be there soon anyway.'" The North Vietnamese mopped up the northern half of the country and then turned south toward Saigon.

Life in Saigon continued at the same hectic pace. The nightclubs, sidewalk cafés, and restaurants were still crowded. Young men and women sped through the streets on their Japanese motor scooters. Some clung to the idea that South Vietnam could survive by holding the delta region, the rich rice basket where the majority of the people lived. But every day, those Americans who remained were approached by Vietnamese friends about being taken out of the country. Under the surface, the city felt the invisible threat of the approaching North Vietnamese Army.

Those who looked to Thieu for leadership found none. He stayed in the presidential palace and was seen only rarely on television. His minister of information met with him to find out what the people should be told.

RIGHT: *On the road out of Pleiku, a boy carries his infant brother on his back as his family seeks safety from the fighting.* BELOW: *March 1975. Under rocket fire from North Vietnamese troops, South Vietnamese marines drop their gear and prepare to swim to rescue ships offshore. The scene is China Beach at Da Nang, where the first American combat soldiers had landed ten years earlier. (AP/Wide World)*

But Thieu did not bring up the subject, and the minister "didn't dare to . . . talk about things the president might not like or agree with."

Any last hopes for the survival of a smaller South Vietnam ended with the battle of Xuan Loc (pronounced Swan Lock), a tiny provincial capital only thirty-eight miles northeast of Saigon. If it fell, the main road to Saigon would be open. On April 9, rockets began to fall on the city, and 40,000 North Vietnamese troops attacked. Five thousand ARVN soldiers fiercely defended Xuan Loc. They fought valiantly for twelve days before they were overwhelmed in what was to be the last battle of the war.

On April 10, President Ford had asked Congress to approve emergency aid of $1 billion to South Vietnam. Congress refused to send more money in what was by now a lost cause. All we could do now was rescue as many people as possible. There were still many Americans in Vietnam —embassy staff, military advisers, civilians administering aid programs, employees of American businesses, Red Cross workers, and members of religious groups who still wanted to help the people of South Vietnam. In addition, there were many Vietnamese who had worked for the Americans and were sure to be on the execution lists of the Viet Cong.

LEFT: *Refugees choke the roads all over South Vietnam as they flee the advancing North Vietnamese troops.* BELOW: *April 1, 1975. An American official punches a man trying to board an overloaded evacuation plane leaving Nha Trang, South Vietnam. (The Bettmann Archive)*

American ships steamed toward the coast of Vietnam. Aircraft carriers brought cargo planes to take people out of the country. But the American ambassador, Graham Martin, delayed the evacuation, fearing it would trigger the kind of panic that had seized Da Nang.

On April 21, the day that Xuan Loc fell, President Thieu stepped down. In a tearful television speech, he blamed the Americans for his failure. He left the country, and most of his generals fled as well. According to one report, Thieu left with several tons of gold to ease his retirement.

On the morning of April 27, rockets fell onto downtown Saigon—the first since the cease-fire. More than 500 homes were destroyed and 5,000 people were left homeless by the fires that followed. North Vietnamese troops had reached the outskirts of the city.

On April 28, General Duong Van Minh became president of South Vietnam—the same General Minh who had led the coup against Diem eleven years before. The United States believed he could make a deal with the North to bring about a truce. Instead, Minh appeared on television and announced that the Americans would have to leave the country within twenty-four hours. After twenty years, our ally was now kicking us out.

The following day North Vietnamese artillery opened up on Tan Son Nhut Airport. Their shells damaged the runway and made it impossible for planes to land. There was now no way out of Saigon except by helicopter. Ambassador Martin was approached by Major General Homer Smith, who threatened that if the evacuation did not begin now, "We're going to look pretty stupid or pretty dead." Martin finally agreed. The radio station began to play "White Christmas"—the signal that all Americans should gather at the embassy.

Everyone knew what it meant, and the embassy became a madhouse. At least 10,000 Vietnamese surrounded it, hoping to find a seat in one of the helicopters. Marine guards used their rifle butts to smash the fingers of those trying to climb the ten-foot-high wall. Americans in the crowd tried to push their way through.

Inside, telephones rang endlessly in empty offices. Smoke wafted through the halls as secret records were burned. But in the haste to get away, the embassy's computer records were left intact. These records contained the names of Vietnamese who had served as American agents. Later, they would suffer when the enemy tapped into the computer.

Ed Bradley, a CBS correspondent, had fought his way inside the embassy. Down a long corridor, he saw a room where clerks were burning millions of dollars in American money to keep it out of enemy hands. Space on the helicopters was too precious for mere money. Bradley reported that he had finally found "the light at the end of the tunnel."

The helicopters were slow in coming from the aircraft carriers in the South China Sea. Starting around three in the afternoon of April 29, they began landing on the roof of the embassy and a few other buildings in Saigon. At the embassy, when the choppers were full of people, pilots tested the load by lifting off a few feet. Then, if the copters could still fly, they shouted, "Put some more on!" Every ten minutes all that afternoon and night, the jammed helicopters took Americans and some lucky Vietnamese to safety.

The ambassador came out at about 4:45 on the morning of April 30. He climbed into a helicopter, leaving behind only a few civilians and ma-

By April 29, 1975, the only way out of Saigon was by helicopter. Here, an American helicopter crewman helps evacuees up the ladder on top of a Saigon office building. (The Bettmann Archive)

rine guards. Crowds of people now broke into the embassy compound and began looting the offices. The marines dropped tear gas into the elevator shafts to keep them off the roof. The last group of marines had to wait two hours for their helicopter. One of them said, "We had faith. 'The Marines won't forget us,' we kept telling each other. . . . It was mayhem down below. The embassy compound looked like it had undergone a nuclear attack." Finally the helicopter came, and the last Americans left Vietnam. As the chopper flew away, the radio buzzed and a voice from one of the offshore ships said, "What kind of pizza do you want?"

Four hours later, a tank smashed through the gates of the presidential palace. Men jumped out and raised the Viet Cong flag over the palace. They had reached the end of the Ho Chi Minh Trail. South Vietnam's twenty-one-year history was over.

Sitting atop their Russian-made tank, jubilant soldiers wave the Viet Cong flag in the courtyard of the presidential palace in Saigon on April 30, 1975, the day the South finally fell to the North. (The Bettmann Archive)

CHAPTER THIRTEEN

"I Finally Got My Parade"

This wedding ring belonged to a young Viet Cong fighter. He was killed by a Marine unit . . . in May of 1968. I wish I knew more about this young man. I have carried this ring for 18 years and it's time for me to lay it down. This boy is not my enemy any longer.

—Note left at the base of the Vietnam Veterans Memorial, Washington, D.C.

AFTER the fall of Saigon, South Vietnam's last leader, Duong Van Minh, called all South Vietnamese soldiers to lay down their arms. Saigon's radio station announced that the city was now called Ho Chi Minh City. All of its homes should display the Viet Cong and North Vietnamese flags. The city's tailors set to work making them.

In Hanoi, the news was greeted with an outpouring of joy. Fireworks were set off, and people swarmed through the streets, weeping and laughing. It was springtime, and the peach and cherry trees had just opened their blossoms—to Vietnamese, the annual sign of rebirth and hope.

But peace did not bring prosperity. As Pham Van Dong admitted some years later, "Waging a war is simple, but running a country is very difficult." Vietnam became poorer while many Asian countries such as South Korea and Singapore experienced enormous economic growth. Many people believe that these countries owe their success to the Confucian values of hard work and education. Although Vietnam shares these values, its Communist system failed to bring prosperity to its people.

Nor did the end of the war mean an end to suffering. North Vietnam forcibly reunited the country, shoving aside the members of the Viet Cong's Provisional Revolutionary Government. More than one million former South Vietnamese army officers and government officials were herded into "re-education camps." Here they were forced to do hard labor and to learn

A farmer drives his cart past a relic of the war—a wrecked U.S. tank left behind by retreating South Vietnamese troops. (AP/Wide World)

the ways of communism. Conditions were harsh, and many suffered from malnutrition. Tens of thousands were still in the camps as late as 1988.

In the years since the war's end, hundreds of thousands of people have fled Vietnam—a mass exodus that goes against all the traditions of Vietnamese history. Even former members of the Viet Cong—betrayed by the North—found that life under the new Communist government was miserable enough to make any escape attractive.

Most of those who left tried to cross the South China Sea in small fishing boats. They became known as "boat people." Some gave all their possessions to anyone who promised to get them out of the country. But many of the boats were so overcrowded that they sank. Others were attacked by pirates who stole what little the refugees had brought with them, and often killed or enslaved them. No one knows how many boat people died in the attempt to find freedom.

Those who reached port found that they were unwelcome. Few countries in the area wanted the burden of feeding and housing the boat people. Sometimes they were herded into temporary camps. In a few places, they were actually forced back out to sea. The prime minister of nearby Singapore said, "You've got to grow calluses on your heart or you just bleed to death."

Canada, Australia, the United States, and some European countries agreed to accept some of the boat people as immigrants. The United States

"Boat people" fleeing Vietnam's Communist government on a dangerously overcrowded boat. All 162 of these refugees made it to safety, but many others did not. (K. Caugler, United Nations High Commission for Refugees)

has taken in hundreds of thousands of them, more than any other country. But there are many still in refugee camps in the Far East.

Another tragic legacy of the war are the thousands of children whose fathers were American soldiers. Some soldiers married the Vietnamese women who bore their children, but often they were not allowed to take their families with them when they left Vietnam. Some husbands later managed to have their families sent back to America. Others forgot about them.

Throughout southern Vietnam today, these orphaned children beg in the streets. They are easily recognized by the American features inherited from their fathers, both black and white, and most Vietnamese shun them. Nguyen Yen, a sixteen-year-old girl who made it to the United States, recalled her third-grade teacher in Vietnam telling her over and over, "Go back to your country."

In 1987, Congress passed the Amerasian Homecoming Act which allows many of these children to come to the United States. Most have not found their fathers. Some have been adopted by American families; others are as unwanted here as they were in Vietnam.

After the fall of Saigon, Americans turned their backs on Vietnam. It was not a war we wanted to remember. The divisions it caused within the country were too strong and too bitter. Perhaps the hardest thing to deal with was the fact that we had lost—for the first time in American history. This country spent at least $150 billion on the war. More than 58,000 Americans were killed and over 300,000 wounded. Their sacrifice, like that of the French at Dien Bien Phu, seemed to have been for nothing.

To the veterans who served in Vietnam, this public silence caused additional pain. There were no welcome-home parades for the returning vets, as there had been after World War II. Many vets were insulted by total strangers as they set foot once again on American soil. Veterans were feared and avoided. People had heard about the horror of My Lai, and it rubbed off on all veterans. Some called them "baby killers."

A hero's welcome is not only a way of thanking soldiers. It shows that those at home approve of what the soldiers had to do in battle. It helps to heal the wounds and ease the guilt of killing. There was no such approval for the Vietnam vets. David Donovan spoke for many of them when he wrote:

I felt my country didn't give a damn about me or the sacrifice I and thousands of others [had made] in their name. . . . It was not unreasonable for a man to figure that his country owed him at least a little respect, a little thanks for the trouble, a little pat on the back for the effort. But thanks and respect were not available, not this time around.

The Vietnam vets' homecoming was more jolting because it was so sudden. The vets left, as they had arrived, one by one. When a man's 365-day tour of duty was up, he was yanked out of combat, leaving his buddies still fighting. Vietnam vets could be in the jungle one day and back in an American city the next. This was totally different from the experience of veterans in previous wars. They had returned home together, usually on ships. They had time to unwind and prepare for civilian life.

Without such preparation, many Vietnam vets experienced problems at home. Their families thought they had changed—the result of facing ever-present danger and death. Wives found that their husbands jumped when they heard loud noises and sometimes woke from nightmares of death in Vietnam.

Some combat veterans suffered from what was called post-traumatic stress disorder (PTSD). PTSD took many forms. A veteran might feel panic or rage for no apparent reason. Some experienced severe depression that kept them from working, feeling love or joy, or finding any purpose in life. Though some were helped by treatment, many were never able to resume normal lives.

Many veterans could not talk about their experiences. Guilt and anger were bottled up inside of them. They had been sent to fight communism, but found that the enemy included old people, women, and even children. Though very few veterans had taken part in anything like the massacre at My Lai, many remembered the bodies of civilians killed by American bombs and artillery. Others felt guilty because they had survived while their buddies had not. For them, Vietnam remained a haunting memory.

Of course, many veterans also bore the scars of war on their bodies. Of the 300,000 wounded veterans, many never fully recovered. Thousands had lost arms and legs or been blinded. Many still remain in veterans' hospitals.

Returning veterans also found it difficult to find jobs at home. The money spent by the United States on the war hurt the economy. During the 1970s, there were fewer jobs for everyone, and veterans were often the last people to be hired. Arthur Woodley, a black Vietnam veteran, said:

I can't speak for other minorities, but living in America . . . is a war for survival among black folks. And black veterans are being overlooked more than everybody. We can't find jobs, because nobody trusts us. Because we killers. We crazy. We went away intelligent young men to do the job of American citizens. And once we did, we came back victims.

In 1979, one Vietnam veteran, Jan Scruggs, decided that there should be a memorial to those who had died in the war. He formed a committee to raise money to build it, and before long Americans responded. Many donations came with notes like one that read simply: "Our son did not come home to us." The U.S. government donated a prominent spot near the Lincoln Memorial for the site.

On Veterans Day weekend in 1982, the memorial was dedicated. People came from all over the country—parents, wives, and friends of the dead, as well as veterans themselves. Seeing the memorial was a heart-wrenching experience for them. They searched the wall for the names of friends and relatives. Finding them, they wept, but knew that at last there was a place of honor for those who gave their lives in Vietnam.

On that Saturday afternoon, a parade of 150,000 people marched through Washington toward the memorial. Many veterans wore their old combat fatigues. As David Donovan recalled:

I finally got my parade. . . . On November 13, 1982, after more than ten years of waiting, the American Army of Vietnam moved out for its splendidly ragtag parade down Constitution Avenue. . . . Men, women, and children were cheering and waving flags. The most common cheer was "Welcome home! Welcome home!" . . . the tears kept filling my eyes, but this time not from sadness—it was from pleasure and immense relief. A parade! For me. A great weight was lifted from my shoulders.

The war affected the United States in ways that are still being felt today. Before Vietnam, Congress usually followed the lead of presidents who wanted to send American troops to foreign lands. The Constitution makes the president the commander-in-chief of the armed forces. But it also wisely divides the war-making powers, giving only Congress the power to declare war. In the Vietnam years, presidents used army, navy, and air force in a full-scale conflict without a formal declaration of

war. So there was no real debate over the wisdom of fighting in Vietnam. This was one reason why Congress passed the War Powers Act in 1973. The act gave Congress a way to keep presidents from involving the country in another Vietnam and sending more and more troops without knowing exactly what we were fighting for.

The war also changed the feelings of the American people toward their government. In the past, the majority of Americans tended to believe what their elected leaders said. Vietnam showed that that trust was not always justified. The credibility gap remained after the war was over. To this day, Americans in general are more distrustful of government than they were when John F. Kennedy took office in 1961.

Today the United States is more reluctant than before to send its armed forces to fight in foreign countries. When such situations arise, the first question is often: Could this turn out to be another Vietnam? This attitude is called the Vietnam syndrome. It caused Congress to hold back funds in

Maya Lin

Like the war, the Vietnam Veterans Memorial became a controversial issue. A nationwide contest was held to find a design. The judges chose the entry of Maya Lin, a twenty-year-old architecture student at Yale University. She had designed what seemed like the simplest of memorials: a black granite wall bearing the names of all Americans who had died in Vietnam.

Many people objected to the design, calling it a "black gash of shame." Maya Lin explained that to her, black was a soothing color and that the polished black granite would act like a mirror to reflect the images of those who visited. People who looked at the wall would see themselves, the living, as part of the memory of the dead.

Lin also designed the wall to be a journey for the living to take. The gradual slope downward leads people into a valley of death and then rises again into the light. "You have to walk out and leave it in the end," she said. Her intention was to help ease the grief people felt at seeing the name of a loved one.

People who opposed the design thought it conveyed no idea of the heroism and bravery of the veterans. They were not ready to accept something so unusual as Maya Lin's design. Finally, the committee decided to compromise by erecting a flagpole and a conventional statue nearby showing three veterans.

But today, those who go to the memorial hardly notice the statue. The wall itself is the most visited monument in Washington, and its base is lined with mementos—letters, medals, photographs, any tangible reminder of those who had lived, been loved, and now were dead. This practice began on the very first weekend of the memorial's dedication, and it continues to this day. Nothing like it occurs at any other war memorial. Each evening guards at the memorial collect the mementos and store them. Someday, they will be displayed in a museum near the wall.

the early 1980s when President Reagan wanted to aid anti-Communist rebels in the Central American country of Nicaragua. Congressional leaders remembered that this was how we became involved in Vietnam.

Military leaders are also affected by the Vietnam syndrome. The experience of the war hurt their pride. It took the army in particular a long time to repair the loss of morale caused by the war. Many of today's high-ranking officers served in Vietnam and have not forgotten the lessons they learned there. They want to make sure that in any future wars, the goals are clear and the country is united behind them.

In the movie *Rambo*, Sylvester Stallone played a bitter Vietnam veteran who is sent back to rescue American prisoners. He asks his commander, "Are we going to be allowed to win this time, sir?" His question reflects the feeling that the United States could have won in Vietnam.

Americans by the millions went to see *Rambo*. Perhaps it was so popular because it gave audiences a chance to see us "win"—even though it was only a movie.

What were the mistakes we made in Vietnam? The biggest error was in thinking the United States was so powerful that it could achieve any goal. We had defeated the Nazis and the Japanese in World War II. Vietnam was a much smaller and weaker country. Most Americans thought we could certainly bend its people to our will. Even today, years after the end of the war, people still find the outcome difficult to swallow.

We did not realize that the Vietnamese were willing to take casualties and accept punishment that Americans would not. The Vietnamese had a cause—independence. The war was one more battle in their 2,000-year history of fighting foreign domination. To them, it was worth their lives. In thinking that Vietnam was only a war against Communist aggression, we failed to understand why the Vietnamese were fighting. They felt just the way we would if another country invaded ours.

In such a war, Americans would, as John F. Kennedy had said, "pay any price, bear any burden." But for the United States, Vietnam was not that kind of war. Americans would not pay that price in a war whose purpose seemed unclear, against an enemy that was no threat to us.

The protest marchers in the United States did, it is true, do much to turn the country against the war. Those who were serving in Vietnam felt betrayed by the marchers. But the majority of protesters were not demonstrating against our soldiers; they were trying to keep more of them from being killed. If the Americans were in Vietnam to defend freedom, then the freedom of Americans to protest had to be defended as well.

Finally, there is the issue of what role the media played in the outcome of the war. Television and newspaper coverage of the war made Americans uneasy. But in fact, the journalists were reporting honestly and fairly what they observed. Documents such as the Pentagon Papers show that in most cases, it was the government that lied to Americans—not the reporters. One of our most precious rights as Americans is the freedom of the press to write about, and to criticize, the government.

In 1987, former Secretary of Defense McNamara broke his silence on the war. He said that he knew as early as 1966 that the United States could not win. Of the 58,132 names listed on the Vietnam Veterans Memorial, more than 50,000 died *after* McNamara knew the war was a losing cause. Who served the country better—the reporters who described our mistakes and defeats, or the government officials who lied about the war so that more Americans could be sent to Vietnam?

Ever since the war's end, there have been questions about the MIAs—Americans reported as missing in action. These men are listed on the Vietnam Veterans Memorial with a cross before their names. The plan is that if any of them return alive, the cross will be circled. So far, there are no circles.

Yet many people believe the MIAs are being held against their will. Some have claimed that Americans have been sighted in Vietnam, Cambodia, and Laos. In the early 1980s Colonel Bo Gritz, a former Green Beret, led a secret mission into Indochina to search for Americans who were still held prisoner. He found none.

There were many reasons for a man to be reported as missing. In some cases, planes went out on missions and never returned. It was assumed that they had crashed and their crews were either killed or taken prisoner. Some of these missing men did return when North Vietnam gave back prisoners in 1973. Others were never accounted for. In the 1980s, the remaining MIAs were officially declared dead, but their friends and relatives still hope.

The United States has tried to get Vietnam to provide more information on the MIAs. This has been made difficult by the fact that we do not formally recognize Vietnam—we send no ambassador there, and we do not trade with that country. And the United States never sent Vietnam the aid that Nixon promised—because North Vietnam violated its agreement not to invade the South.

After World War II, the United States helped the nations it had defeated. Today West Germany and Japan are two of our strongest allies. Vietnam has not been so fortunate. Though our bombers devastated both North and South, we have made no attempt to aid the nation's rebuilding.

Some American veterans have returned to Vietnam in recent years. They visit old battlefields, trying to come to grips with their past. The Vietnamese welcome such visitors, treating them as ex-foes who fought bravely. William Broyles, one such returning American veteran, said:

I went back to find a man I never knew—my enemy. I went back to find the piece of myself I had left there, and to try to put the war behind me. . . .

For millions of Vietnamese who fought on our side, the end of the war has meant suffering, imprisonment, exile, even death. But for the North Vietnamese and for most of the Viet Cong and the people of the South, the end of the war has meant they could live and work in peace, if not in freedom and prosperity.

The dead are buried. Life goes on. It is not a society I could live in, but I was not on the winning side. They won, we lost, and it is their country now.

The United States has not been able to rid itself of the memory of Vietnam. The divisions in this country have not fully healed. Long after the fighting has stopped, the pain of the Vietnam War is still with us. There has been no end to the hostility between the United States government and Vietnam.

To finally put the war behind them, Americans must find a way to end it, in Nixon's words, "with honor." We might begin by trying to understand the Vietnamese and their history—and the part we have played in it. American pride has been stung by our defeat in Vietnam. No one likes to recall the only war we ever lost. But by learning why we lost, we can discover something important about ourselves. Only then will we know why there are 58,132 names on a black granite wall in our nation's capital.

Glossary

Agent Orange: Chemical used in U.S. defoliation program; later proved harmful to civilians and military personnel who were in the areas sprayed.

Amerasians: People of mixed American and Asian descent.

ARVN (Army of the Republic of Vietnam): South Vietnam's army.

Attrition: Strategy of warfare that involved killing enough enemy soldiers to make the cost in lives too great for the enemy to continue fighting.

Baby boomers: Those Americans born between 1945 and 1960; the largest generation in American history.

Blacklist: List of people suspected of being disloyal to the United States; those on the blacklists lost their jobs or were prevented from working in certain industries.

Boat people: Refugees who fled Vietnam by boat after the war.

Body count: The number of enemy soldiers killed in battle; used by the United States to measure progress in the war.

Buddhism: A religion practiced by about 75 percent of Vietnamese people. Buddhists believe that people's souls are reborn again and again, until they achieve perfection.

CIA (Central Intelligence Agency): One of several U.S. government spy agencies; one of its functions is to carry out activities that the government does not want publicly known.

Communism: A social, political, and economic system in which, theoretically, people would share equally in the nation's wealth. In practice, though, Communist governments have harshly repressed their people to maintain control.

Confucianism: A philosophy based on the teachings of the Chinese scholar Confucius. It stresses the importance of education, family relationships, and the duties that each person in a society owes to the others.

Counterculture: The various beliefs and practices of those Americans in the 1960s who questioned the generally accepted ideas and values of American society.

Counterinsurgency: A plan for defeating Communist rebels, or insurgents, by arming and training villagers to defend themselves and, at the same time, giving them economic aid.

Coup d'état: A usually violent attempt to overthrow a government or ruler by a small group within that government.

Credibility gap: The feeling of many Americans that their government was not telling the truth about the progress of and reasons for the war.

Culture brokers: Those Vietnamese who served the French colonial government as interpreters and officials at the village level.

Defoliation: The attempt to eliminate enemy hiding places in jungles and grasslands by using airplanes to spray the land with poisonous chemicals, or herbicides, that would destroy plant life.

DEROS (Date of Expected Return from Overseas): The date on which an American soldier would have completed his one-year service in Vietnam, and thus be due for reassignment in the United States or other noncombat zone.

Dinh: Central building of Vietnamese villages; it housed the village guardian spirit and also served as a meeting place.

DMZ (Demilitarized Zone): An area around the

17th parallel in Vietnam where no military forces were allowed to enter.

Domino theory: First publicly expressed by President Eisenhower, the idea that if South Vietnam fell to Communist rebels, then neighboring countries would in turn fall, like a row of dominoes when the first one is toppled over.

Dove: Anyone, but especially an elected government official, who opposed or questioned the U.S. government's involvement in the Vietnam War.

Draft: The forced recruitment of civilians into the armed services; on his 18th birthday, every American male had to register for the draft, and could be called up anytime afterward.

Draft card: The card that was mailed to every American male to show that he had registered for the draft; he was required to carry it for identification purposes.

Draft resister: Anyone who actively opposed the draft system by refusing to register, burning his draft card after registration, fleeing to another country, or refusing to serve if called.

Fragging: The practice of killing a superior officer or a sergeant by troops who felt the superior was unnecessarily risking their lives; named after the fragmentation grenade, which was often the weapon of choice in fraggings.

Geneva Accords: Agreements made at the Geneva Conference of 1954. Among other things, they ended the fighting between French and Viet Minh forces and temporarily divided Vietnam along the 17th parallel.

Green Berets: Members of the U.S. Army Special Forces, nicknamed for their distinctive headgear.

Guerrilla war: A type of warfare in which rebel forces are part of the civilian population and try to wear down a larger, well-armed enemy force by means of ambush, hit-and-run attacks, and terrorism.

Hawk: Anyone, but especially an elected government official, who fully supported the U.S. government's involvement in the Vietnam War.

Ho Chi Minh Trail: A network of camouflaged jungle paths—later a paved highway—through Laos and Cambodia; used by North Vietnam to send supplies and troop reinforcements south.

Lurp: Military slang for long-range reconnaissance patrol, in which a group of soldiers spent days or weeks searching enemy-held territory.

MACV (Military Assistance Command—Vietnam): Name for the U.S. military headquarters in Saigon, South Vietnam, set up in 1962 to supervise the increasing number of American military advisers in Vietnam.

Mandarins: Educated Vietnamese who served the emperor as government officials and scholars.

Mandate of heaven: In Confucianism, the power that gave the emperor, or any ruler, the right to rule.

McCarthyism: The practice of making public accusations of disloyalty to the U.S. government without proof or sufficient evidence; named after Senator Joseph R. McCarthy, who built his political career on such accusations in the late 1940s and early 1950s.

MIAs (Missing in Action): U.S. military personnel who were never accounted for.

Monsoon: The season when heavy rains fall in southern Asia, marking the time for rice planting.

Napalm: Jellied gasoline enclosed in bombs dropped from airplanes; because it stuck to whatever it landed on when the bomb exploded, it caused serious burns.

Nationalism: The spirit that unites a group of people who believe that they are all part of one nation and motivates them to be free and independent of outside control.

NLF (National Liberation Front): The political organization of the Viet Cong, which operated as a "shadow government" in areas of South Vietnam under Viet Cong control.

NVA: The North Vietnamese Army, which frequently fought alongside the Viet Cong but remained a separate organization.

OSS (Office of Strategic Services): A U.S. government agency created during World War II to collect information and assist guerrilla forces fighting the Japanese and Germans; forerunner of the Central Intelligence Agency.

Pentagon Papers: A secret report and collection of memos that describe the history of U.S. involvement in Vietnam from 1954 to 1968.

PTSD (Post-Traumatic Stress Disorder): A mental illness that afflicted some American veterans of the Vietnam War. Its symptoms sometimes did not appear until years after the veteran returned home.

Punji sticks: Sharpened bamboo sticks placed by guerrilla forces in camouflaged holes and just below the surface of rice paddies.

Puppet: A government or head of government which has no real power and which follows the orders of another nation.

Rolling Thunder: Campaign of continuous bombing of North Vietnam by the United States from March 1965 to November 1968.

Sanctuaries: Areas of Cambodia and Laos used as "safe havens" by Viet Cong and NVA troops. Because these countries were officially neutral, U.S. troops could not enter them.

17th parallel: A temporary dividing line under the terms of the Geneva Accords; it ultimately became the border between North Vietnam and South Vietnam.

Short-timer: An American soldier who had only a short time left in Vietnam before being reassigned to the United States or to a noncombat zone.

Tet: Vietnamese new year holiday; a time when many Vietnamese like to return to their home villages.

Tunnel rats: U.S. military personnel whose job it was to crawl through enemy tunnel complexes in search of Viet Cong.

Viet Cong: Guerrilla forces that sought to overthrow the South Vietnamese government. Also known as VC, Victor Charles, or Charlie.

Viet Minh: A military and political organization set up by Ho Chi Minh in 1941 to unite Vietnam's people in their struggle for independence. It included both Communist and non-Communist Vietnamese.

Vietnamization: President Nixon's policy of gradually withdrawing American troops and shifting the burden of the fighting onto the South Vietnamese army.

War matériel: Weapons, ammunition, and other equipment needed in warfare.

Watergate: General name for the many scandals associated with the Nixon administration that eventually forced President Nixon to resign in 1974.

Further Reading

Boettcher, Thomas D., *Vietnam: The Valor and the Sorrow,* Little, Brown (Boston, 1985). Heavily illustrated, with many interesting sidelights. This is the best general history of the war by one who served in the military forces there.

FitzGerald, Frances, *Fire in the Lake: The Vietnamese and the Americans in Vietnam,* Atlantic–Little, Brown (Boston, 1972); paperback: Vintage (New York, 1973). Written while the war was still going on, this book helped turn American public opinion against the war. It contains much information about the history of Vietnam and American involvement there.

Karnow, Stanley, *Vietnam: A History,* Viking (New York, 1983). Karnow's book was the basis for the PBS television series, and is the best general history by a journalist who covered the war.

Maclear, Michael, *The Ten Thousand Day War,* Avon (New York, 1981). A lively and readable book covering the war from 1945 to 1975. Written by a Canadian journalist, it too served as the basis of a television series.

Santoli, Al, *Everything We Had,* Random House (New York, 1981); paperback: Ballantine (New York, 1982). Interviews with thirty-three American soldiers who fought the war. There are many oral histories of the war—this is the best.

Sheehan, Neil, *A Bright Shining Lie: John Paul Vann and America in Vietnam,* Random House (New York, 1988); paperback: Vintage (New York, 1989). Though this is a biography of an American officer who died in Vietnam, it illuminates the history of the war to 1972.

Terry, Wallace, *Bloods,* Random House (New York, 1984); paperback: Ballantine (New York, 1985). Gripping and very graphic stories of black American soldiers' struggles at war and at home.

Truong Nhu Tang, *A Vietcong Memoir,* Harcourt Brace Jovanovich (San Diego, 1985). A fascinating story by one of the leaders of the people the United States was fighting in Vietnam.

Walker, Keith, *A Piece of My Heart,* Presidio Press (Novato, Calif., 1985); paperback: Ballantine (New York, 1987). Vivid interviews with American women who went to Vietnam both as civilians and as military personnel.

The Wall: Images and Offerings from the Vietnam Veterans Memorial, Collins (New York, 1987). Deeply moving photographs of scenes at the Vietnam Veterans Memorial.

Index